Paul's Social Network: Brothers and Sisters in Faith
Bruce J. Malina, Series Editor

Titus

Honoring the Gospel of God

Ken Stenstrup

A Michael Glazier Book

LITURGICAL PRESS
Collegeville, Minnesota

www.litpress.org

A Michael Glazier Book published by Liturgical Press

Cover design by Ann Blattner. *Saint Paul*, fresco fragment, Roma, 13th century.

Excerpts from documents of the Second Vatican Council are from *Vatican Council II: The Basic Sixteen Documents*, by Austin Flannery, OP © 1996 (Costello Publishing Company, Inc.). Used with permission.

1	2	3	4	5	6	7	8	9

Library of Congress Cataloging-in-Publication Data

Stenstrup, Ken.
    Titus : honoring the Gospel of God / Ken Stenstrup.
        p.   cm. — (Paul's social network : brothers and sisters in faith)
    "A Michael Glazier book."
    Includes bibliographical references and indexes.
    ISBN 978-0-8146-5287-9
    1. Titus, Saint.   2. Bible. N.T. Galatians—Criticism, interpretation, etc.   3. Bible. N.T. Corinthians, 2nd—Criticism, interpretation, etc. 4. Paul, the Apostle, Saint—Friends and associates.   I. Title.

BS2520.T58S74   2010
225.9'2—dc22

                                                          2009026669

"Paul's partner and co-worker Titus has been an underappreciated figure in New Testament studies. Ken Stenstrup's analysis of Titus is thus welcome. By explaining in simple terms the first-century Mediterranean context—such as cultural presuppositions concerning hospitality, gift giving, and collectivistic behavior—Stenstrup brings Titus to life, especially as he is portrayed in Galatians and Second Corinthians."

> —*Thomas D. Stegman, S.J.*
> Associate Professor of New Testament
> Boston College School of Theology and Ministry

"Ken Stenstrup's volume on Titus ably recognizes and addresses the cultural distance that separates many contemporary readers from the world of the New Testament epistles. His attempt to breach this gap is two-fold. First, drawing from a "generational approach model" offered by the social sciences, he locates the writings of the New Testament, including those which speak to Titus' character and role as Paul's fellow missionary, within the prevailing tendencies of different developmental periods in early Christianity. Second, he introduces readers to anthropological understandings of how persons in Paul's day viewed themselves and others as collectivist persons, perceived change and causality, pursued and granted honor, and engaged in conflict. Stenstrup's book offers readers a helpful illustration of how the use of social scientific concepts and models can enable readers to bridge the gap between past and present and open up fresh ways of understanding the New Testament documents, the characters they portray, and early Christianity."

> —*Karl Kuhn*
> Associate Professor of Religion
> Lakeland College

"An incisive and cogent writer, Ken Stenstrup provides his readers with models that unravel the cultural norms, perceptions, and values that shaped first-century Mediterranean persons such as Titus. The author's skillful analysis of how hospitality, gift-giving, and boasting functioned in the cultural world of Titus provides information essential for a fair reading of the New Testament. As one who successfully resolves sensitive issues within Jesus groups, Titus emerges as an innovative and respected change agent, one of Paul's most trusted partners in his proclamation of the gospel of God."

—*Joan C. Campbell*
Atlantic School of Theology
Halifax, Nova Scotia

"Stenstrup's rigorous application of the 'generational approach model' in the analysis of New Testament documents mentioning Titus maintains the high quality of books in this series. Titus as presented in fourth generation documents (Luke-Acts and the letter to Titus) is very different from the 'real' Titus, co-worker of Paul, presented in second generation documents (Galatians and 2 Corinthians). Earlier believers routinely recast or re-presented their ancestors for the edification of their own generation. By his thorough examination of this process, Stenstrup offers contemporary believers a solid method for and classic examples of actualizing or contextualizing biblical texts in a new generation."

—*John J. Pilch*
Visiting Professor of Biblical Literature
Georgetown University, Washington, DC

For Nick and James

This is more or less PG-13 so it may be a couple of years.
But when the time comes, I hope you enjoy reading this
as much as I enjoyed writing it.

CONTENTS

PREFACE

Human beings are embedded in a set of social relations. A social network is one way of conceiving that set of social relations in terms of a number of persons connected to one another by varying degrees of relatedness. In the early Jesus group documents featuring Paul and coworkers, it takes little effort to envision the apostle's collection of friends and friends of friends that is the Pauline network.

This set of brief books consists of a description of some of the significant persons who constituted the Pauline network. For Christians of the Western tradition, these persons are significant ancestors in faith. While each of them is worth knowing by themselves, it is largely because of their standing within that web of social relations woven about and around Paul that they are of lasting interest. Through this series we hope to come to know those persons in ways befitting their first-century Mediterranean culture.

Bruce J. Malina
Creighton University
Series Editor

ACKNOWLEDGMENTS

This book began with my review of notes taken as an undergraduate at Creighton University. Another student there once suggested that with my interest in the Bible I might enjoy a class with Bruce Malina. Thirty years later that remains one of the biggest understatements I've ever heard. My thanks to Bruce Malina and all of those who have contributed to the Social Science Task Force of the Catholic Biblical Association over the past decades. I also thank my colleagues at Saint Mary's University of Minnesota for the sabbatical that allowed me the time to write this book, and especially Dr. John Reed for his initial reading of and feedback on an earlier draft of this manuscript. Finally, I thank those at Liturgical Press, especially Hans Christoffersen and Lauren L. Murphy for their help in improving subsequent drafts.

INTRODUCTION

A search of comprehensive reference works on the Bible would probably reveal information about two first-century persons named Titus. One was the son of Vespasian, the Roman emperor remembered for having begun the siege on Jerusalem. Before completing that siege, Vespasian was proclaimed emperor and the task of completing the campaign against Jerusalem was handed to his son Titus. By all accounts, Titus made his father proud. The Israelite temple system in Jerusalem was effectively destroyed around AD 70.

Another Titus had been to Jerusalem decades earlier accompanying Paul and Barnabas. Through the celebration of his feast day, contemporary Christians might know this Titus as a disciple or secretary of Paul or as an example of chastity. What follows is more specifically focused on what can be known about Titus from the documents of the New Testament. These documents indicate that Titus was a very important person in service to the early Jesus groups associated with Paul in the late 40s and the mid-50s. In one place Paul sums up his importance by stating that Titus is "my partner and fellow worker in your service" (2 Cor 8:23). Altogether there are only a dozen or so other statements in the New Testament that refer directly to Titus. But, the quality of these descriptions provide a good deal of information about Titus, his relationship with Paul, and their mutual efforts to promote their shared understanding of what new things the God of Israel was doing for his people.

Before unpacking these ancient descriptions, the rest of this introduction will explore some basic views about the Bible and how the New Testament documents may or may not impact us. In particular, the effort is made to distinguish how an academic reading of the documents found in the Bible might be distinguished from perhaps a more familiar reading of these documents in the context of a tradition's worship.

For many in the United States, the Bible is a principal source for faith. It is important whether it is read or not.[1] How Christians understand the Bible and particularly the New Testament is often shaped or at least influenced by their participation in a denomination. Many denominations utilize a lectionary, a book that lists or includes biblical passages to be read within worship. Focused on celebrating the life, death, and resurrection of Jesus, Christian lectionaries for weekly liturgies progress through the gospels almost in their entirety every three years. Much to the surprise of some, however, no other documents from the Bible are ever read completely. The criteria for choosing non-gospel readings have to do with a text's ability to correspond to a key theme, topic, or term thought to be highlighted in the gospel selection. So, while some sections are read more than once a year (e.g., sections of 1 Cor 15), about half of the material from the non-gospel texts of the New Testament is not included in the Lectionary.[2]

Material about Paul's associate Titus serves as a typical example. Roman Catholics who attend Mass daily but never encounter the Bible outside of liturgy would hear about half of the letter to Titus. Written in the late first century, this letter depicts Paul commanding Titus to attend to matters yet to be accomplished on the Mediterranean island of Crete (Titus 1:5). By contrast, the Lectionary provides only two brief examples of what Paul and Titus actually did. And neither of these is read on any day of obligation. The Tuesday Mass of the eleventh week of Ordinary Time presents Paul's praise for those in Macedonia who, despite trying circumstances, had made significant contributions to a collection for the poor in Jerusalem. This reading also notes the interest in having Titus help the Corinthian community further their efforts for the collection (2 Cor 8:1-9). The next year (non-gospel Lectionary readings for weekday liturgies alternate), specifically the Wednesday reading of the twenty-seventh week of Ordinary Time, presents Titus accompanying Paul to Jerusalem (Gal 2:1, 2, 7-14). As the verses in the parentheses indicate, not all of Paul's depiction is read. The omitted verses (3-6) note that Titus was not compelled to be circumcised and that Paul was not all that impressed with those the Jerusalem community perceived to be leaders.

While the process used for selecting texts for the Lectionary is far from clear, it seems likely that issues from the omitted verses were not considered important or appropriate complements to the gospel reading, Luke's account of the Lord's Prayer (Luke 11:1-4). Since homilies may or may not relate to these Lectionary readings and since some of those delivering them are required to complete only a handful of introductory level courses on the Bible (the requirements for most permanent deacons are even less), worshipers would not necessarily find out why the topic of circumcision was an issue in letters from Paul or, for that matter, how or why Luke's presentation of the Lord's Prayer differs from Matthew's portrayal (Matt 6:5-13). Nor in the alternate year would one necessarily hear about the issues involved with the collection Titus was to assist, or why Paul would have been concerned that not all in Jerusalem would be able to receive this gift without incident (Rom 15:25-33). So, worship settings do not necessarily provide an adequate setting for uncovering the best data available about such persons like Titus or Paul.

Beyond determining what from the Bible is read or how it is to be explained, doctrinal positions can also shape one's understanding of the Bible. For example, most Christian denominations would be able to articulate an understanding of the New Testament's references to Jesus' brothers and sisters. The passage in question might be something like Mark 6:3 where people from his hometown ask, "Is not this the carpenter, the son of Mary and brother of James and Joses and Judas and Simon, and are not his sisters here with us?" Although one will not find any specifically named siblings in the Gospel of Luke (8:19-21), Matthew's gospel includes Mark's question nearly verbatim (13:55-56). Paul never mentions a group of siblings, but he does have a similar reference. Prior to his description of a trip to Jerusalem with Titus, Paul's letter to the Galatians refers to an earlier trip where Paul had met "James, the Lord's brother" (Gal 1:19). For a tradition that would define Mary as a perpetual virgin, such brothers and sisters would necessarily be understood to have come from some other mother. One's heritage might suggest Joseph had children from a prior marriage or that these brothers and sisters were persons from Jesus' extended family. Reading the same documents, other traditions that never recognized any state of perpetual virginity might promote the understanding that Jesus was born of a "virgin," meaning that Jesus had no earthly father. But, then, invoking a notion similar to the section of Matthew 1:25 that states Joseph "knew her not until she had borne a son," a tradition might hold that, subsequent to the miraculous birth, Mary had other children with Joseph.

Accounting for the perspectives of Christians not associated with a denomination is a bit more difficult. Such persons and groups seldom provide an explicit statement about how the Bible is viewed or understood. Some nondenominational groups, however, promote the concept of a foundational or gateway Scripture. Those who have seen "John 3:16" flashed at a sporting event or plastered onto a billboard or bumper of a car might be at least partly familiar with this perspective.[3] As a kind of cornerstone or foundational Scripture that presumably captures some kind of basic meaning or message for the entire Bible, one might accept the insight from this verse and then move on to encounter the thousands of other verses in the New Testament. But without any explicit consideration for how Scripture is to be read, it is difficult to know how one would reconcile the above verse suggesting "whoever believes" in the "only son" finds "eternal life" with other verses like 1 John 3:16 ("By this we know love, that he laid down his life for us; and we ought to lay down our lives for the brethren") or 1 John 3:17 ("But if any one has the world's goods and sees his brother in need, yet closes his heart against him, how does God's love abide in him?").

Whether one is more familiar with the Bible as presented in a Lectionary or as presented in a few of its more popular verses, those who read the Bible in its entirety not only consider more data about Titus and other associates of Paul, they also more readily realize that the Bible is not like contemporary literature. One might notice its rather un-American views about what it means to be a male or a female or how one discerns if marriage is appropriate (1 Cor 7:7-9). The Bible offers strange views of when it is appropriate for a public stoning (John 8:7) or why wives should be "subject" to their husbands (Eph 5:24). The Bible offers different notions about newborns and why it is only after the seventh day that males from the hill country of Judah and Galilee would be named and circumcised (Luke 1:59; 2:21). Those who wrote and initially read the documents of the Bible seem to hold different notions about peace, or what the Gospel of Matthew meant when it portrayed Jesus assuring those around him that he came not to bring peace but the sword (Matt 10:34; cf. Luke 12:51 where "sword" is replaced with a less violent "division"). While it may appear rather odd to contemporary readers, Matthew's initial audience had little difficulty understanding what Jesus meant when he told a man who had recently lost his father that he should "leave the dead to bury their own dead" (Matt 8:21-22). These initial readers understood what was involved in tithing or, for that matter, why someone would sell "everything" and give as needed or hand everything over to one who redistributed it as there was need (Acts 2:44-45 and 4:34-35). They even understood the integral role of slavery in their economy well enough to be able to accept the early Jesus movement's notion that those called to be in Christ as slaves needn't mind their status (1 Cor 7:21).[4]

Since all cultures share notions of self, others, the physical world (nature, time, and space), and how everything is held together (besides the Divine, even random chance is relevant here), it can be tempting for anyone today, Christian or not, to assume that the Bible reflects contemporary views of marriage or peace. And since the Bible is part of Christian origins, it might also be tempting for one to think that the Bible matches modern Christian notions about sin, slavery, salvation, or the Holy Family. At a very broad level it does. These were concepts in antiquity and they are still concepts in our modern world. But it is also true that those who wrote about these issues nearly two thousand years ago were not like our contemporary neighbors. They held specifically different concepts about males, females, marriage, sin, economies, salvation, peace, etc. Concerned about addressing the tensions that can arise as modern readers encounter ancient texts, some denominations began to formulate constructive solutions. For example, beginning with a document called *Divino Afflante Spiritu* (1943) and then again in *Dei Verbum*, a 1965 document from the Second Vatican Council, the Roman Catholic Church articulated broad approaches for understanding Scripture and tradition as sources of insight for salvation. While there are several aspects to *Dei Verbum* that would prohibit most traditions from adapting it entirely, the general method for reading the Bible continues to be broadly adapted by many interpreters. Essentially, modern readers are asked to consider the Bible in light of the context of those who wrote it and the initial readers. The rationale for this approach is articulated here in part:

> Seeing that, in sacred scripture, God speaks through human beings in human fashion, it follows that *the interpreters* of sacred scripture, if they are to ascertain what God has wished to communicate to us, should carefully *search out the meaning which the sacred writers really had in mind, . . . attention must be paid . . . to* literary genres *. . . [and] circumstances of . . . time and culture."* (*Dei Verbum* 12; emphasis added)

In general, this book investigating Titus takes up the challenge to consider Titus in light of the entire collection of New Testament documents and, equally as important, to pay attention to the circumstances of time and culture, not despite but because of distances between "us" and "them." In order to appreciate Titus fully, we must first decide what data from the New Testament is most relevant. Then we must begin to find a way to negotiate our recognition that humans are broadly the same, yet, at the level of culture and meaning, often hold important differences that can create difficulties for interpreting these ancient data. To help achieve these objectives, this study will rely on insights from social-scientific methods. As noted in a previous volume in this series, the social sciences seek to provide some of the "context that is necessary for readers who don't share the language, culture, or perspectives to interpret the texts."[5] In order to provide such context, a social-scientific approach utilizes "perspectives, theory, models and research of the social sciences."[6] This study of Titus will utilize several models from previous social-science studies. Such models were often initially developed with no specific interest in the cultures presented in the Bible. But as time-tested models, these have been adapted to the biblical data in a number of more recent studies. (Some of these are listed in the endnotes and bibliography.)

A model merely describes how a system looks and works given the data available about that system. By analogy, one might consider the use of physical models of the solar system often used in elementary or grammar school. Constructed out of foam balls, string, and wire, these simplified (sometimes movable but seldom to scale) models offer, at the very least, a simplified view of the solar system. They seldom include asteroids or any depiction of atmospheres, but they do allow students new to science the ability to visualize our planet as the third in a series of eight or, if you are a traditionalist, nine planets from the sun. In later grades, students are asked to replace or complement these physical models with more conceptual models that better allow for one's perception of scale or the orbits of the various planets. These may serve as a touch point for more abstract discussions about how the Copernican model eventually replaced the formerly received Ptolemaic model as a tool that better accounted for the increasing data being made available by new technologies like the telescope.

Models utilized in the social sciences are likewise simplifications of more complex reality. Like the models of the solar system, they help us think about the data available. More specifically, social-science models help us think about and understand what people have done and continue to do in their interpersonal relationships. More abstract models may even be able to represent human behaviors in such a way that they generally account for a majority of persons, not simply the behavior exhibited by one's own culture. The value of such cross-cultural models for those who read the Bible is that they offer a way for a contemporary reader in the United States to consider the Bible as a collection of documents from an ancient and foreign world. As they account for differences in time and circumstance, models offer a process for negotiating the respective differences between cultures and help to create a kind of bridge over which these distances and distinctions can be appreciated in ways that sometimes go beyond the perspectives of the various traditions. Foremost, the use of such models allows for replication or refinement by others utilizing the same or similar method.

This study of Titus will begin with a description of a generational response to a new phenomenon and will discuss how groups evolve through time and how change agents function as persons who initiate and seek to sustain such groups. It will also draw on studies of ancient gift giving and explore the importance of hospitality for first-century persons like Paul and Titus. By the end of this book we might consider what it means to say that Titus was a collectivistic person competent to maintain ascribed honor in roles including hospitality and gift giving that contribute to the integrity of fictive kin relationships in groups anticipating the theocracy of a God articulated as patron. Most people who hear or read the Bible today within worship or devotional settings do not care to talk about it or its characters through the lens of a model expressed through such jargon. And, in general, that would seem to be a good thing. It is no more suggested that modern interpreters who employ such models consider praying to a "patron" than it would be suggested that those studying our solar system think of the earth or other planets having a support wire that extends from the South Pole to a base that exists below the sun (physical model) or that there are little dashes in space so that the planets know where to orbit (conceptual model). As a tool for learning, however, the process of engaging conceptual models about groups, change, honor, hospitality, or patrons helps us understand what the ancient writers intended and meant as they communicated to others like them, but not so much like us. Those typically more focused on the Bible as it is used in liturgy or as a conversation piece for contemporary ethics might find these social-scientific tools very helpful when considering the data provided in all documents from the Bible. And, if one's interest is ultimately devotional or tied into postbiblical theologies, one would hopefully consider the results of this exploration and return to participate in that devotion or tradition with insightful questions, the foundation of any vibrant and healthy theology. Denominations will continue to shape doctrine with attention to the more immediate need to communicate the essentials of what is necessarily sufficient for the salvation of contemporary Christian believers. By contrast, this book simply explores some of the basics of what can be known about Titus relative to the context of his time.

The general flow of this book is from the broad to the more specific. So, some of the initial and basic information might be review for some readers. Unlike most academic study designed with appreciation for skills that advance sequentially along with an increasing interest in the topic, most of those who begin the study of the Bible do so with a wider range of previously acquired skills and dispositions.[7] As an academic perspective interested in utilizing methods that can ultimately account for all of the data available, the insights from social-scientific studies will sometimes complement previously acquired skills and dispositions. At other times, however, there may seem to be a tension. This study is not interested in describing how all traditions evolved from the Bible. It is more narrowly focused on presenting Titus as a single character named only in some of those documents.

Chapter 1 begins with an overview of the New Testament. Utilizing a generational approach model, the variety of New Testament documents will be assessed with a view to those that are particularly useful for a social history of Titus. Also included is a brief overview of how persons like Paul and Titus related to small groups that made up the early Jesus movement and how these groups formed and evolved. Chapter 2 is more focused on the cultural perceptions of persons like Paul and Titus. This chapter draws some of the basic distinctions that exist between the ancient Mediterranean culture of Titus and Paul and the contemporary culture shared by many readers of this book. The chapter ends with a discussion of how Paul came to honorably respond to the gospel of God within that culture. Such background sets the stage for how one like Titus would have perceived Paul and his gospel. Chapters 3 and 4 then demonstrate how the basic insights provided in the first two chapters can be combined with documents that mention Titus, specifically the letter to Galatians (chapter 3) and the Second Letter to the Corinthians (chapter 4). As a summary, a concluding chapter (5) presents differences brought out in some of the subsequent traditions about Titus, especially those presented in the letter to Titus. The chapter also includes an overview of others who furthered traditions about Titus for their own time.

CHAPTER 1

Titus in Paul's Network

This chapter begins with an overview of the New Testament documents. These documents are next related to one another through a "generational approach model." The model provides a few general characteristics of the various groups that produced these documents and thus allows us to consider which documents provide what types of data about Paul and Titus. The chapter concludes with a general overview of how Paul and associates like Titus typically interacted with others within the network. Included here are considerations of how Paul functioned as a change agent, how Titus and others worked with Paul to adapt this change, and how small groups develop over time.

Overview of New Testament Documents

In order to appreciate Titus as an associate within the early Jesus movement, it will be necessary to understand how that movement related to and operated with its principal figure, Paul. We know these people primarily through the New Testament, a collection of twenty-seven documents produced around the northeastern region of the Mediterranean between the mid-first and early second century (ca. AD 50–120). Because they primarily describe the life of Jesus, some might assume the gospels are the oldest documents in this collection. The earliest, however, the Gospel of Mark, was written about AD 70, more than a decade after the latest letters written by Paul and his associates, and nearly four decades after the death of Jesus (ca. AD 30). The other three gospels were written even later, at least a decade after Mark (ca. AD 85).

Fourteen of the twenty-seven documents in the New Testament mention Paul and his associates. Since Paul never met or traveled with the earthly Jesus, there is little difficulty in understanding why Paul or associates like Titus or Timothy are never mentioned in the four gospels. It is not entirely clear, however, why Paul or his associates are not mentioned much in other New Testament documents.[1] Thirteen letters have come to have Paul's name attached to them. The narrative known as the Acts of the Apostles also describes Paul and some associates. In time, the "letter" to the Hebrews became yet another document associated with Paul. Modern critical studies of vocabulary, style, and especially ideology and subject matter have demonstrated that Paul did not write Hebrews or, for that matter, six of the thirteen letters ascribed to him and others.[2] Initially then, one could classify the New Testament documents referring to Paul and his associates into three types: authentic letters (Romans, Galatians, 1 and 2 Corinthians, 1 Thessalonians, Philippians, and Philemon); pseudepigraphic letters, that is, letters once thought to be from Paul but now considered to be "as if" from Paul (Colossians, Ephesians, 2 Thessalonians, 1 and 2 Timothy, and Titus); and the Acts of the Apostles.[3]

In general, the authentic letters present Paul and his cowriters as collaborative correspondents concerned with sustaining the integrity of the groups with which they and associates like Titus were connected.[4] Though this collaboration can be overlooked or undervalued, the tendency to write collaboratively parallels the tendency to work collaboratively.

When compared to these authentic, collaborative letters, the letters written after Paul's death (ca. AD 62) and the narrative

Acts of the Apostles offer differing and sometimes contrasting portrayals of Paul and his associates.[5] Like any document in the New Testament, Acts is broadly concerned with articulating what God had done and would yet do. But Acts articulates these actions through a recognizable agenda. Those who are mentioned as carrying on after the resurrection are presented in stereotypical fashion, acting with "one accord" (Acts 1:14; 15:25; see also the similar "together" 2:1, 46; 4:24; 5:12). Removed from the context of Paul and Titus by more than thirty years, Acts often presents Paul as one very much like others acting in one accord. Written about the same time as Acts, the pseudepigraphic letters lack a familiarity with the problems or challenges faced by respective audiences of the authentic letters. The letter to Titus, for example, portrays Paul as a less intimate, unilaterally commanding figure concerned with only generic matters. Titus is presented as one who must be directed through some very basic issues for the group in Crete.

The Generational Approach Model

This diversity of documents and perspectives might prompt certain questions: If Paul's letters are the oldest documents in the New Testament, why did it take so long for people to write about Jesus? Why didn't more New Testament documents mention Paul and other members of the network like Titus? Why do some documents present Paul as a unique apostle while others present him as another like the Twelve?

Many modern introductory textbooks address these concerns by noting how various texts are distinctive types of literature produced at various times following the death and resurrection of Jesus. These are important factors. But further insight into the circumstances surrounding these documents can be gained through the use of a generational approach model.[6] As used here, a "generation" signifies any distinct group that can be arranged sequentially in a line of descent from the person or event of focus. Through consideration of many groups responding to a situation of "significant and irreversible change," the model broadly notes the following characteristics: A first generation is that group that has directly experienced a "significant and irreversible change" in its social situation. Such a drastic modification makes any interest or effort to sustain the former status quo, the old ways, impossible. By contrast, the second generation is characterized as in tension with the first generation and typically seeking to ignore many dimensions of that first generation. A further shift or swing happens as the third generation then seeks to remember or reclaim what the second generation ignored or forgot. In contrast to the second generation, the third generation is characterized as proud of the first generation and seeks to recapture this initial generation forgotten or ignored by the second.

Applied to the data of the New Testament, the first generation is made up of those with Jesus. Anticipating the arrival of God's kingdom, this generation experienced the significant and irreversible change, the crucifixion and resurrection of Jesus. By contrast, the second generation that ignored most of Jesus' life, deeds, and many features of the first generation is that of Paul and his network. The third generation is then comprised of those who, with the writers of the gospels of Mark, Matthew, and John, were concerned about remembering what the second generation had ignored. At the same time these third-generation groups were establishing roots in the initial generation, there appeared subsequent generations relative to Paul and his associates. These are the writers and communities reflected in the pseudepigraphic documents mentioned above. The data of the New Testament suggest a fourth generation relative to the group with Jesus. This is reflected in the two-part work of the Gospel of Luke and the Acts of the Apostles, documents that tie together the slightly diverging views of each preceding generation into a more seamless progression.

The First Generation

The initial group called by Jesus worked to promote the proclamation of an imminent theocracy to be established in and around Judea and centered in Jerusalem. In social science terminology, the first generation technically operated as a faction, a group of people brought together by some person for a specific period of time in order to carry out a specific purpose.[7] Jesus had been responsible for recruiting those who were to bring about that goal of God's kingdom and, while alive, continued to serve as a central person for both the inner circle of twelve disciples and for the others embedded in Jesus during his journeys throughout Galilee and, to a lesser extent, in Judea. The disciples of Jesus were his helpers, persons who came to adapt Jesus' concern to bring the kingdom.

There are no documents written by members of this first generation. Later generations, however, generally portray the goals of this initial generation in terms similar to the following excerpt from the Gospel of Mark. About three and a half decades after the death and resurrection of Jesus, Mark reports that after the arrest of John the Baptist, "Jesus came into Galilee, preaching the gospel of God, and saying, 'The time is fulfilled, and the kingdom of God is at hand'" (Mark 1:14-15). While brief, this highly compacted saying indicates that the generation with Jesus operated with two fundamental assertions. First, various Judean (Pharisees, Sadducees, etc.) and Israelite expectations about when, why, how, and where God would act were now irrelevant. The time of God's action was here and now. Second, what God was bringing was a kingdom. Such a theocracy, or "God rule," would render the current kingdom under the human-divine Caesar irrelevant, at least in Galilee and Judea. Of course, such language was insurrection. And under Roman control, the fate of most influential insurrectionists was death. While these nuances are not explicit in the writing of Mark, there would have been little surprise to find this gospel portraying the death of Jesus through a Roman-sanctioned public execution known as a crucifixion.[8]

With the death of Jesus, those who had been working toward the reception of a theocracy transformed from a faction into a "political religious party."[9] Survivors necessarily began to function in ways paralleling the Pharisees, Sadducees, or Essenes, other parties who claimed to have the understanding of how Israel's identity and actions should be manifest. It appears that some of those who had accompanied Jesus remained in or, considering John 21, soon returned to Jerusalem to live for some time there after his death. Paul notes two meetings in Jerusalem with survivors of this first generation. The first meeting with Cephas (Peter) and James occurred about six years after the death of Jesus. A subsequent meeting with those two and another, John, occurred later, nearly two decades after the death of Jesus (ca. AD 49).[10]

Given their appreciation of God's having raised Jesus from the dead, their idea of a theocracy could still be anticipated. But, obviously, the means to that end would no longer be through the faction associated with the earthly Jesus. Perhaps the theocracy was thought of as coming from above through the one God had raised from death, Jesus the Christ. Not a last name, the Greek term transliterated into English as "Christ" was a translation of the Judean term "Messiah." Anyone who held this title was recognized as having been anointed for a particularly divine purpose, to carry out a particular task.[11] As Christ, Jesus' task would have been to bring the theocracy to those Israelites who had now come to anticipate a reprieve from God's punishment for the first failed theocracy under the line of David (ca. 586 BC).

Specifics about the kingdom's arrival and its composition would continue to be nuanced long after most of those from the first generation had passed away. The latest biblical view from the fourth-generation book of Acts depicts the risen Jesus being asked if it was time for the restoration of the kingdom of Israel (Acts 1:6). Jesus' response is that "It is not for you to know times or seasons which the Father has fixed by his own authority" (Acts 1:7). The third-generation Gospel of Matthew presents the earthly Jesus announcing the "Son of Man" will come in glory and with angels. With that arrival, some who apparently never even knew or proclaimed Christ would be chosen for their acts of compassion while others would be sent to a fiery demise (Matt 25:31-46). In contrast to this third generation's kingdom to come, the second generation anticipated an imminent return of Christ.

His return would bring salvation for those who believed in Jesus as one once dead but now risen (1 Cor 15:2). One second-generation letter suggests that at least some in Thessalonica had become concerned with the heavenly kingdom for those who had passed away. Paul writes that those bound to be with Christ in heaven will meet the Lord upon his descent. And those who have already passed will precede those in Christ who yet remain (1 Thess 4:13-18). Since Thessalonica is about two thousand miles from Judea, it would seem that the second-generation view of the return did not perceive this as an event limited to those who made the effort to travel to or remain in or around Jerusalem.

The Second Generation

The activity of the second generation is best presented by their letters, the earliest written documents from the New Testament. Consistent with the broader model, this generation held certain tensions with the first generation and tended to "ignore" or managed to forget most of the previous generation's defining characteristics. (Many of these will be reclaimed by the next or third generation.) Beyond their view of when the kingdom will come, second-generation persons like Paul and Titus tended to ignore the first generation's initial interest in transforming Israel. Rather, second-generation letters portray a consistent concern to sustain Diaspora Israelites (in Galatia, Corinth, Philippi, or Thessalonica) despite a world of powers that would threaten both the honor of these groups and their physical well-being. These letters stress that those in Christ must continue to support one another in spite of these threats from beyond the group. The second-generation groups are not directed to replace, defeat, or transform these realities, but they are to anticipate God's delivery or salvation from them for those who are "in Christ." Thus, in distinction to the first-generation group, which was oriented toward an objective political theocracy, the second-generation groups are more social activity groups. Their principal function is to keep the group together and await God's delivery. As noted above, this delivery will occur in a way similar to God's delivery of Jesus from the power of death (1 Cor 15:12-58). In the mean-while, early Jesus movements associated with Paul, like other second generations, had to figure out how best to inhabit two worlds. Generally, Paul seems to have advised that people were to sustain the protocols of respect for those involved in the more direct, day-to-day control of this world (Rom 13) even while a fuller life in Christ was expected. These distinctions do not in-tend to imply that the behavior and identity of the Pauline groups did not matter or had no impact on outsiders. They merely point out that the primary target of change was not a transformation of Roman-controlled politics, but the continual transformation of those in Christ. Pieces of this transformation can be seen in the letters' descriptions of grace or, more specifi-cally, God's gifts manifest within the respective groups (see, e.g., 1 Cor 12–14). It is for this transformation that Titus and others serve.

Another part of the transformation anticipated for these second-generation groups was the ability to suspend at least some of the customs and requirements that may have been ap-propriate prior to God's newest revelation, God's raising Jesus from the dead. Said another way, second-generation persons like Paul and Titus were not at all interested in sustaining all the customs and behaviors apparently still considered requisite by some of the survivors of that first generation. Circumcision, dietary restrictions, and certain calendar observations are noted as expressions appropriate enough for Israelites leading Judean lifestyles. But these were no longer necessary features of a life in Christ. To the contrary, the second generation was clear that if they hadn't already become irrelevant to those Diaspora Isra-elites who long ago found themselves living great distances from Jerusalem, they were now irrelevant given the new thing God was doing.[12] Paul and those with him did not find the earthly Jesus irrelevant, but they did find the risen Christ more relevant, indeed, crucial.

As an extension of this perspective, one can note how Paul and his cosenders only occasionally mentioned fundamental or core traditions that are traced to the earthly Jesus. Paul's mention

of a Eucharist meal (1 Cor 11:23-24), a meal that Mark and Matthew will describe as a re-signification of the Passover meal, and
his note that "the Lord commanded that those who proclaim the
gospel should get their living by the gospel" (1 Cor 9:14) [13] are
two noteworthy exceptions to the otherwise general tendency
to avoid mentioning the concerns of the generation before. In
other words, the letters from Paul and his associates have little
information about the life and times of Jesus, son of Joseph. They
are more focused on what God's raising of Jesus meant for non-
Judean, more generally Hellenized (Greek) or Diaspora Israelites. These are the Greeks Paul speaks to who had, over the
course of centuries, come to share fewer and fewer behaviors
with those Israelites closest to the temple.[14] Paul's concern with
contacting this specific group of Israelites is especially drawn
out in his recollection of a trip to visit with Cephas and others
in Jerusalem. The letter to Galatians notes the distinction that
while Paul was to focus on non-Judean Israelites, others like
Cephas and James were to concern themselves with the Judeans
(those in and around the Jerusalem temple) who had come to
appreciate the vision of God raising Jesus from the dead even
while retaining some of the customs more typically associated
with the temple (Gal 2:7-8; also, see below, chap. 3). Decades
after this letter to the Galatians, the fourth-generation book of
Acts will portray Paul and others taking their message about
Christ to Israelites only to be rebuked. In response, Acts has Paul
turn his efforts primarily to non-Israelites. (This shift is specifically described on three different occasions: Paul in Antioch,
13:46; Corinth, 18:6; and Rome, 28:17-28.) At the time of Luke's
writing, the temple in Jerusalem had been destroyed for at least
a decade and a half. Prior to its destruction, however, Paul and
associates like Titus were primarily concerned with non-Judean
Israelites.

The Third Generation

The third generation relative to Jesus sought to revitalize some
of what the second generation had ignored or did not bother to

include. While Paul and his cosenders happened to mention that the Lord thought it was okay for those who proclaimed the gospel to receive support for their effort, Paul and his cowriters provided very little information about what Jesus said or did. They never mention Jesus being named or baptized, they never describe much about his presence in and around the Jerusalem temple for study, prayer, participation in festivals, or, for that matter, Jesus' efforts to make whole those persons whose illness or abnormalities would have excluded them from interacting with the temple-mediated God. While Paul, Titus, and other associates held their own views on the importance of dietary or other behaviors typically associated with those who lived in the area around Jerusalem, third-generation gospels generally portray Jesus re-signifying the meaning and importance of dietary and calendar matters. It isn't what goes in that can defile so much as what comes out (Matt 15:11). The bread and wine are no longer about a past exodus but about him (Matt 26:26). While the death of Jesus is mentioned here and there (2 Cor 4:10; Gal 3:1) as a precursor to the more often mentioned resurrection, the second-generation letters include little elaboration of Jesus' last days in Jerusalem, being arrested, or publicly dishonored. And while second-generation texts repeatedly communicate Jesus as one raised by God, these documents make no mention of the events that took place in the garden after his death. For example, there is absolutely no consideration of Mary Magdalene's contact with Jesus, a feature of the postresurrection events shared by all four gospel accounts (Matt 28; Mark 16; Luke 24; and John 20). We know these events and many others only because of the efforts of the third-generation authors who were concerned with including what the previous generation had ignored.

While recapturing what had been ignored, each of the gospels was being written with attention to concerns generated by its particular circumstances around AD 70–85. For example, while the scribes and Pharisees are far from ingroup characters in Mark's gospel, the Gospel of Matthew demonstrates an elevated contempt for this party of Judeans. More than a decade after the destruction of the Jerusalem temple, Matthew's gospel presents

Jesus not only as a kind of quintessential next chapter in Israel's story but also as a specific counter to the heinous Pharisees. Matthew's contempt for the Pharisees is perhaps best seen when Jesus teaches his disciples to pray. The fourth-generation author of Luke is not devoid of criticism of the Pharisees. But he presents a softer Jesus teaching his disciples the Lord's Prayer simply because some wanted to learn to pray like the disciples of John the Baptist (Luke 11:1-4). By contrast, Matthew presents Jesus teaching the very same prayer in distinction to both the stereotypically hypocritical Pharisees who seek honor by praying in public and the equally stereotyped non-Judeans (Matt 6:5-13).

The Fourth Generation

The fourth generation is foremost characterized by its awareness of previous generations, especially as it tries to tie these together into a reasonably seamless trajectory. This perspective is clear in the prologues or dedications given at the beginning of the Gospel of Luke and the Acts of the Apostles. Written by one who had been following the events for some time, Luke's gospel is to be an orderly account considerate of previous narratives (Luke 1:1-4). Similarly, the book of Acts begins by noting its interest in carrying on with the perspectives from the "first book" and further relates Jesus to the larger process that began in Scripture (the Old Testament) and continued on through the first decades after the resurrection of Jesus. Sometimes this concern with tying it all together appears to have required Luke to remove or rewrite events or subject matter that was seen to be unnecessarily controversial. For example, the introduction noted that Luke does not include the specific names of persons said to be the brother of Jesus (James in the second generation) or his siblings (Joses, James, Judas, and Simon in the third-generation gospels). The fourth-generation Luke portrays Jesus saying only that those who hear and do the will of God are "my mother and my brothers" (Luke 8:19-21; cf. Matt 12:46-50; Mark 3:31-35). While difficult to prove a negative, it is possible and productive to note patterns. And when one isolates both the material left out of Luke and what is found only in this gospel, there is a recognizable agenda. The two-part work presents a progression from Genesis through to the events following Jesus' death and resurrection in its own way, seldom addressing tensions that exist between it and earlier writings. Removed from the second generation of Paul and his associates by at least thirty years, the fourth-generation Acts of the Apostles presents Paul as one linked to Peter. With others, both Paul and Peter are linked with Jesus through healings and proclamations before both the common and elite.[15] The net effect and, hence, the suggested agenda, is to bring the entire phenomenon (regardless of persons involved) together under the direction of Holy Spirit and acting with one accord.

Many of the pseudonymous authors writing as if they were Paul similarly demonstrated an interest in reclaiming roots in a first generation. But again, when compared with the authentic letters, it is clear that these later letters recapture the second generation with both significant and subtle changes. These changes have long been thought to reflect the later writer's interest in depicting Paul as if he were still alive and still responding to the questions and concerns that came only decades after his death. In other words, the later writers portray Paul responding to the contemporary questions of the later author's day, not those of the second generation. In general, the later documents present the collaborative Paul as a more remote and unilaterally commanding leader. We will see that while the authentic letters present Titus as very much his own man, the later generations portray Paul commanding directives to Titus that are to be followed without question. Many of these directives would have been so obvious to anyone who spent time with Paul that there would have been little motivation for the authentic Paul to have belabored these basic matters to a trusted associate like Titus.

Applied to the data of the New Testament, the model of generational change over time allows contemporary readers to appreciate the diversity of documents and points of view presented within the New Testament. It also shows how these points of view can change slightly over time and demonstrates how one's appreciation for context can influence one's understanding of the data in these documents. For example, when a person or event is discussed in multiple documents, the generational approach model presents a way for a modern reader to negotiate these respective portrayals. As this study presents the portrayal of Titus in Galatians and 2 Corinthians in distinction to the portrayal in the letter to Titus, the model will allow for an appreciation of how this figure could be recast or re-presented for a subsequent generation. Finally, and most important for this study, the model points out that anyone concerned about better understanding Titus as one of several in Paul's network would do well to begin with insights gathered from the second-generation letters.

An Overview of Paul and His Closest Associates

Beyond a framework within which to consider the variety of New Testament documents written over time and from different perspectives, the social sciences also provide tools that can help one consider the basic social interaction going on within this all-important second generation of writing. For example, Paul is often described as an apostle. He describes himself as such, sometimes specifically noting he had been called by God (1 Cor 1:1; 2 Cor 1:1; Gal 1:1; etc.) and set apart for the gospel (Rom 1:1; Gal 1:15). Letters from Paul, however, also describe some "brothers" who are "apostles" (2 Cor 8:23, NAB; it is more often translated as "messengers," RSV, NRSV) of those called. In other contexts, those with Paul are referred to as apostles (1 Cor 4:9 and 9:5). Paul is also aware that there had been "apostles" before him (Gal 1:17). Paul seems to include James, the brother of the Lord as an apostle (Gal 1:19) and might also include Junias and Andronicus as apostles (Rom 16:7). Apostles are also associated with being "ambassadors for Christ" (2 Cor 5:20), coworkers (1 Cor 3:9; 2 Cor 6:1), and perhaps even those who respond to the reality of the resurrection of Jesus (Rom 1:1-6). Paul also mentions "superlative apostles" (2 Cor 11:5; 12:11) who would compare themselves favorably to Paul.

Other documents from other generations hold different notions about the role of an apostle. As noted above, later writers present Paul as an apostle who unilaterally orders people like Titus and Timothy to install elders or enforce a group's adherence to generic behaviors. As the third-generation Gospel of Matthew comes to a close, the eleven are sent to "make disciples of all nations," baptize people, and teach them "to observe" all Jesus had commanded (Matt 28:19-20). (While not given the specific title, the Twelve were noted as apostles in Matt 10:2.) With its mission of both the Twelve (9:2-5) and the seventy (10:1-20), the fourth-generation Gospel of Luke might look like it is more inclusive of apostles. Acts, however, depicts a stronger correlation between apostles and the Twelve. These teach and perform "wonders and signs" (Acts 2:43; 5:12). They also receive financial support in order to redistribute it where needed (4:35). They make important decisions (16:4), lay hands on people (6:6), and are noted to be able to give people the spirit through such an act (8:18). From a perspective less focused on the everyday difficulties of groups newly "in Christ" and more on modeling witness (Acts 1:8; 4:33), Paul is characterized as one like others who provide such witness. Such generational and inner-generation characterizations of what an apostle does suggest that another way of characterizing the second-generation Paul would be more insightful than simply calling him an apostle.

As noted above, second-generation writings portray a typical concern with bringing news to others about what God was now doing through the death and resurrection of Jesus. As part of their concern for those who received this innovation, the second generation sought to establish and sustain communication with those adapting this news. Such data suggest Paul and others can be more precisely understood as "change agents."[16] In more modern, individualistic contexts, change agents might be associated with creating a "payback matrix" or leading brainstorming exercises. From a broader, cross-cultural perspective, however, a change agent is anyone sent by a change agency to perform basic tasks that provide information leading to a need for change. In other words, a change agent functions on behalf of another.

First, a change agent develops a need for change. Second, communication between the agent and those adapting the change must be established and maintained. Third, a change agent must be able to diagnose problems or setbacks preventing change. Fourth, the intent to change must be something taken on by the group. In other words, a change agent needs to motivate the group to change. A fifth task is to see that this intent to change is translated into action toward change. Sixth, a change agent must seek to stabilize change and thus prevent discontinuation of the change. With all of the above achieved, the change agent is ready to allow the group to function without the change agent. In other words, the final task of the change agent is to terminate the relationship, to allow the group to function with a clear understanding of itself as a group.

The authentic letters depict Paul and others like Titus as motivated to establish a relationship with groups in order to have them adapt the news of God's new relationship with Israelites made clear through the raising of Jesus from death. As noted earlier, rather than continue the first generation's concern to transform the world into a theocracy, the evidence of the second-generation letters suggests Paul and his associates sought a transformation of the group. Such change could be contrasted with a former life (1 Cor 1:26; 6:10-11; 12:2; Gal 3:23; 4:3, 8-10; Phil 3:7). It could also be characterized as a partial, but not yet complete, transformation to come from God. In the meanwhile, Paul and his associates were intent on sustaining various forms of communication that would help them diagnose and respond to problems. Far from socializing for the sake of socializing, second-generation letters are typically focused on immediate and serious issues that, if left unaddressed, could threaten the stability of the various groups addressed. (Chapter 3 will more fully demonstrate how these threats could impact communication.)

To help in the process of sustaining the best communication possible, Paul sought out the assistance of honorable persons both from within his circle and from the respective groups that were forming in Christ. These persons could be thought of as the first adopters of the innovation. Sometimes, these persons are mentioned by name. Stephanas is remembered as one of the first whose household had received the gospel and continued to live in service to the saints or holy ones chosen by God for this new day (1 Cor 16:15). Chloe is another from Corinth who at least initially played an important role for the success of the innovation (1 Cor 1:11). When communicating through letters, Paul probably relied on trusted others for their delivery. Such persons were probably competent in making sure the letter or information therein was accurately received. The second-generation letters show that these others who worked for the innovation—coworkers and coadapters for the awareness of the new thing God was doing—became an essential part of Paul's work. Somewhat similar to those who were asked to drop everything they had to follow Jesus, some of those who aided Paul would likely have been a more regular part of Paul's circuit. Such persons did not necessarily travel with him constantly (though Timothy did for a time), but they appear to have traveled in his circles and to have kept in contact with the same groups. Rather than persons with official titles, it might be best to think of such persons as holding the interest, ability, and means to circulate with Paul more often than most. These persons probably needed to be capable of conversing with Paul about what was and was not valued for a life in Christ. These persons also seem to have had a degree of sensitivity to and appreciation for the nurturing of a group through its various problems or with its various concerns. Like Paul, such persons must have at least been familiar with the general interest to diagnose problems, solidify the intent to adapt change, stabilize membership (from ingroup tensions), and prevent discontinuance. As dedicated to the goals of the change agency, they were often very much like the change agent, especially as they sought the stability for the groups. In general, they were able to "foster obedience to the demands of the innovation and allay dissonance."[17]

It is possible that one like Titus may have lacked Paul's expertise in using Scripture. It is also possible that few if any of the named coworkers were the recipients of visions like those received by Paul. Yet, what they might have "lacked" was probably more than compensated for by something like a certain social expertise. Perhaps one like Titus was more familiar with the nuances associated with conventions of Greek culture in a particular region. Such familiarity could have served Paul as a bridge to better bonding between himself and a community like that at Corinth. Such bonds would have become indispensable as Paul and others sought to promote continually better reception of the new thing God was doing.

Groups within the Network

The term "group" will continue to be used to describe those with whom Paul and his network associated. This term is preferred because it is broad, referring generically to a small gathering of people who see themselves as a single social entity. The term "church" found in many translations of the New Testament is anachronistic, not appropriate for the time under study. A "church" more like the institution contemporary Christians are aware of was coming, eventually. But for Paul and his initial contacts, the preferred way of referring to the various groups was simply "those gathered."

Generally, small groups follow a pattern.[18] Grounded in the desire for meeting perceived needs or, more generally, change, groups develop through a process of forming, storming, norming, performing, and, eventually, adjourning. In general, the initial stage of forming is characterized by uncertainty as members explore how the group might meet perceived needs. As the various members eventually become more assertive within the group, the storming stage is associated with conflict as various members seek respective needs. At the norming stage, conflicts among members give way to mutually agreed upon behaviors that allow for a more positive reception of membership. Performing is that stage characterized by the group's working together to solve problems. Finally, with problems solved or changes completed, the group can gradually disengage from one another, adjournment.

Contemporary readers can assume there was a stage of forming for the second generation. But details about this stage are infrequent within the second-generation letters. Collectively, the seven authentic letters suggest persons like Paul and Titus found success with groups in relatively larger cities. As hubs for trade, larger cities were suited for the exchange of both goods and information. Given the second-generation sense of urgency to reach as many as possible, it is plausible that Paul and others would have sought out such hubs for their efficiency. The letters of the second generation do not provide the same kind of itinerary as that provided in the fourth-generation book of Acts. These letters, however, do suggest that Paul's efforts to bring the innovation lasted over a decade. Given his contacts with cities like Athens (1 Thess 3:1), Ephesus (1 Cor 16:8), Corinth, Thessalonica, Philippi, and those in the region of Galatia, it is clear that Paul could not have stayed at any one place for extended lengths of time. Other glimpses into the forming stage come from brief asides like those at Philippians 4:16 or 2 Corinthians 1:19. The latter notes Paul did not initially work alone in Corinth. In Philippians Paul notes that he had been supported by the Philippians while working in Thessalonica. Similarly, while working in Corinth Paul relied on support provided from some from Macedonia (2 Cor 11:9). But beyond such brief asides there is very little data about any specific order of initial operations taken on by those who worked with the groups founded by Paul and his associates. What is clear is that these groups came together in response to the gospel Paul and his network worked tirelessly to bring.[19]

Neither are the stages of norming, performing, and adjournment well attested from the second-generation letters. The letters broadly indicate that the groups were to aim at a norm wherein the group behaved in a manner that constantly reflected their awareness of its status in Christ. The majority of issues in these letters, however, are concerned with reacting to the issues of the storming going on within groups and only hint at a future stage of norming. Nor are letters associated with Paul typically about performing. The efforts Paul makes to both explain the meaning of the collection for those in Jerusalem and to move it to completion would be a kind of limited exception. In the end, however, beyond whatever temporary relief it may have provided, the collection is primarily a gesture that will manifest any group's awareness that they are not alone in their appreciation of God's activity in raising Jesus from death. Finally, as Paul began to make plans to journey farther west, he was probably aware that such travel would further separate him from groups to the east. But since Paul does not indicate how long he had planned to be in Spain, it is unclear if he would have viewed this trip as initiating any kind of transition. What is clear is that his plans are all conditional, dependent on the fact that some of those in Jerusalem both accept the gift and allow for his further travels. As groups wait for the God of heaven to act further in a world influenced by the powers that be, the primary concern continues to be how to sustain themselves through problems with perseverance and patience. Factions, misunderstandings, influence from outsiders, and uncertainty all show that storming abounds. Further depictions of this storming stage, as well as descriptions of Titus as one who would qualify as a first adapter or coworker, will be addressed below in chapters 3 and 4. The next chapter provides an overview of how persons like Titus were perceived by first-century peers.

CHAPTER 2

Ancient Perceptions of Persons like Paul and Titus

The introduction noted that some who read the Bible find its documents strange and foreign, seldom like contemporary literature. As a preface to subsequent chapters that focus specifically on the role of Titus as an associate of Paul, this chapter will present some of the basic differences between the world portrayed in the second-generation documents and the world perceived by many of us who today read these documents. Such considerations are important as the documents in the Bible tend to be "high context."[1] Americans reading the Bible today tend to appreciate "low context" texts, texts that include a great deal of descriptive detail, leaving little to the imagination. For example, one could consider wordy legal documents and fast food packaging specifically instructing that frozen pizzas are to be cooked before being eaten or that those buying coffee should know that the coffee is hot. By contrast, biblical documents can be sketchy, relying on generalizations. Even when distinctions are drawn, these can be overlooked by contemporary readers not necessarily familiar with their subtlety. So, while not yet specifically focused on Titus, this chapter contains some rather low-context explanations of how ancient persons like Paul and Titus viewed themselves and their world. The chapter begins with a brief description of the ancient concepts of cause and effect and then continues with perceptions about the person. The former is rather simple. By contrast, the discussion of person can become complex as it moves from a basic description of persons as collectivistic (vs. individualistic) to an appreciation of how collectivistic persons like Paul and Titus sought to sustain honor as they traveled to bring others the news of God's innovation. A model of ancient hospitality is presented as an essential social process for groups that typically didn't welcome change and, as such, were cautious with outsiders. The chapter concludes with an overview of how one in the second generation justified a move from one group to another. While we have no specific data about Titus, we do have Paul's depiction of how he came to be in Christ.

The Perception of Persons in Antiquity

Many today understand events in the world as influenced by a composite of natural law and individual freedom. In other words, the sun "comes out" not because the gods are pleased, but because planets revolve and rotate around our star and/or our atmosphere allows for the sun to be seen, etc. Most Americans do not assume earthquakes damage and kill because God shakes the world. Instead, we understand that the earth's "crust" is not static and that some of us live on or near plates that are slowly pulling apart and every now and then violently lurch only to temporarily resettle again. Children die not because the gods are punishing the parents who must live without them, but because of events that trigger genetic predispositions or because of someone's choice to drive while impaired, etc.

In antiquity, free will and natural law were seldom a part of the conceptual framework. Like other Old and New Testament documents, the second-generation letters presume a world controlled by "personal causality." Essentially, this is the notion that "every effect in life that counts is caused by a person."[2] And in the ancient view, there was a host of "persons" in the world. Some were human, but there were also powers and principalities or "persons" that were nonhuman and sometimes not visible (Gal 4:8). These were thought to exist in a kind of hierarchy composed of spirits or demons, angels, archangels, and other suprahuman persons under God. In our contemporary world it is commonplace to state that some*thing* happened (plates moved, the earth spun, cancer cells were triggered). In a world of personal causality, it could be said that some*one* happened. This notion that if anything happens, a "who," a someone caused it to happen not only accounted for weather, earthquakes, drought, flood, famine, etc., it also accounted for people's behavior. This can be seen in depictions of persons with unclean spirits (e.g., Mark 5:1-20) and in Paul's description of his insight into the reality of Christ (discussed later in this chapter).

The notion that everything and everyone ultimately came from God was complemented by the notion that contact between the divine and the human was often mediated. Prior to Paul's vision of Christ, mediation was thought to come through the Jerusalem temple and the system of priests and rituals associated with the temple. Following the vision of Jesus raised, the principal mediator was Jesus the Christ. With the concern to spread news about this event, Paul sometimes explained Christ as one like a broker, the go-between to serve as a more personal mediator between God and those "in Christ" (e.g., Rom 1:4-5). As those second-generation groups in Christ began to experience some of the gifts from this mediation (e.g., 1 Cor 12–14), Paul and his associates made it clear that it was appropriate for those who received these gifts to praise the one who had given them (1 Thess 5:18; Rom 6:17; 2 Cor 1:11; 4:15). This way of describing how God and Christ related to groups formed by Paul mirrored the patron-client relationships that existed in any person's day-to-day activities.[3] There were no free markets. Exchanges were possible because the elites who controlled all access to services and goods allowed for them. The few elites who held access to goods and services essentially allowed a gift to trickle down as a favor, often translated as "grace" in the New Testament. Typically the elite were not known directly by all those below them. They were, however, knowable through the series of mid-level persons who successively passed things from the elite to those clients whose lives were benefited from such gifts. In other words, some of the favors that initiated with the elite were passed along with the initial one gifted (a client) in turn becoming a patron (giver) for other clients. These exchanges continued until there were no more to receive save the "expendables," persons typically not considered worthy of any client status.[4] The exchange came full circle as clients who received the material or services praised those patrons who provided them. This praise would not be a one-time praise, a simple "thank you," but a commitment to acclaim socially or to honor the status of the giver. Within these interlocking networks, persons were socially related.

While presented here as the rules of the game, these exchanges were all very fluid. A patron could decide to direct gifts elsewhere, and the one gifted could find a more beneficial giver elsewhere. This is what happened when Paul realized that God was acting through Jesus and not the temple. Paul and Israelites like him who came to share news of the innovation suspended such former roles and began to demonstrate a life "in Christ."

The notion of a group of clients sharing the same patron could imply that these clients were expected to behave in similar ways. The book Christians refer to as the Old Testament is full of stories depicting the problems created when Yahweh's people act like the clients of another god (patron). One can see the situation spelled out in the minirecitals of the past presented in Ezekiel 20 or 2 Kings 17. Both sections depict what the patron (God) can and should do when clients (the Israelites) do not behave as expected. Essentially, both documents make it clear that if God was not going to be honored as the ultimate giver of the land, then as punishment, others would control the land that had been promised to the Israelites. With the exception of a brief respite about two centuries prior to the time of Paul, the punishment that had begun with God giving the land to the Babylonians (ca. 586 BC) continued through the current Roman occupation of the land. In Paul's view, however, God's rule could once again be anticipated by those who were aware of God's new activities. Jesus had been given as one allowing for the cessation of God's punishment for the lack of human consideration or praise. And with God's raising of Jesus, it seemed to those of the second generation that the punishment was nearly complete.

Under God as patron, second-generation Jesus groups could see themselves as gifted by God and bonded together as brothers and sisters, members of a pretend, or "fictive," kin group. By contrast, Americans even within a family typically think and behave like individualists. We often perceive the self as a unique person, each a "dynamic center of awareness, emotion, judgment and action organized into a distinctive whole and set contrastively both against other such wholes and against its social and natural background."[5]

Despite the contemporary American comfort with individualism, however, most cultures have been and continue to be collectivistic. Paul, Titus, and others in the network (and, for that matter, most ancient Mediterranean groups) viewed the person as collectivistic. A collectivistic or group-oriented person is one who understands a person as formed by the group. As a collectivistic person, one's motivation is not to further mark the self as unique, but to adapt to the norms of the group and thus embed oneself within the group. In other words, the group determines the person and the person welcomes such formation. For collectivistic persons, the most important groups were those established at birth. And, typically, one's association with these groups remained throughout one's life. Through birth one entered an extended family that, for most, was tied to the land. As members of extended families, persons lived in intimate villages or, within a city, in more intimate ethnic quarters of that city. With a concern to sustain the honor (status) of the group, the interests and goals of the person were often focused on the group's integrity, concerned with observing and sustaining the typicality of the group, that is, concerned with who is in or out of the group. Rather than one's ability to be free or self-reliant, collectivistic persons are concerned with paying attention to the group's norms and, in broader social circles, guarding its name or reputation. Such reputations are often portrayed in the high-context documents of the Bible as static and thus capable of being stereotypically used to identify (and thus distinguish) those in the group from others, those outside the group.

The difficulty for modern readers can be that ancient groups were appreciated at different levels by different groups. We will see this below in Paul's description of his past. As a more immediate example, we might consider that for those in his village, Jesus was the carpenter's son. So when he begins to behave differently, identifying him as such is intended to raise suspicion about his less-than-"carpenter"-group behavior (Mark 6:1-6). Beyond the village, his identity as Jesus of Nazareth told those beyond Nazareth (e.g., other Galileans) that he could be expected to behave like other Nazarenes. Shortly after the arrest of Jesus near Jerusalem, Peter is marked as a Galilean. His denial becomes both a manifestation of his desire to live and, at the same time, a shameful renouncement of his birth-given identity (Mark 14:70; Matt 26:69-75). Paul has similar concerns with identity in his travels throughout the wider Mediterranean. While Paul is concerned with Israelites, he and other Israelites would have been aware of the various subgroups of Israelites. Israelites in and around Judea held on to certain norms that were not shared by Israelites who lived far away from Judea. And at the same time, those within Judea could, if necessary, be distinguished as Pharisees or Sadducees, etc.

As the example with Peter illustrates, an important part of identifying oneself with a group was to be constantly aware of its social standing and to be willing to defend it if it should be challenged. This is the concern with honor. At the time of Paul's writing, honor was a kind of social currency. People like Titus and Paul were constantly concerned for their honor as individuals connected to the larger groups in Christ. Broadly defined, honor is a person's claim to worth along with a social recognition of that worth. In other words, within a collectivistic society, if one claimed to be a 7 (on a scale of 1 to 10) and those around him also saw him as a 7, he would have made a statement that kept his honor intact. If, however, one sought to pass himself as a 9 and those around him only saw a 7, he would have needed to publicly demonstrate how he was a 9 by interacting successfully with other 9 persons. More than likely he would have been reminded of his 7 status through the help of others like him who would have recognized his inflated claim and demonstrated (charitably or otherwise) how he was a 7. If he was not able to interact successfully with other 9s or able to take the group's reminder that he was a 7, he could have been shamed into submission. Were any minority of persons to entertain his claim to be a 9 while the majority insisted he was a 7, these would have been in jeopardy of being labeled "fools," themselves shamed for their inability to accept the collectivistic decision of the majority of the group.

While one's status or honor was typically "ascribed" or given at birth, there are, of course, rare instances where honor beyond that given at birth was acquired or gained. But unlike a contemporary notion of a person "climbing through the ranks," significant changes to status (honor) in antiquity were typically only granted by others (personal causality). As persons like Paul and Titus traveled into and further from Palestine, they probably experienced how something that was honorable for a group in one area or region was not all that important for another group in another region. We will consider the example of circumcision below, but a more immediate example might be the various roles of females. In Judea, Israelite women were typically portrayed as most appropriately embedded in a male. Thus, their "honor" was to show respect for that male. For father and/or brother, such respect included keeping one "fit" for marriage. Once married, such respect was ultimately expressed in bearing one's spouse a male heir. Beyond Judea, however, other norms allowing women more freedom were appropriate, especially for Roman women. Paul's ability to appreciate local distinctions was an important part of his success. It is also clear that for Paul and others of the second generation, such distinctions were ultimately meaningless given the new understanding of Jesus raised from death.

The Practical Challenges of Traveling to Create and Sustain New Groups

As noted above, Paul's vision of Jesus raised by God led eventually to his desire to share this insight with others interested in the God of Israel. So, as a change agent, one interested in creating a need for change, Paul was often on the move, particularly interested in going to places where others had not already established the gospel (Rom 15:20).[6] Others like Titus and Timothy were also on the move. While these agents of change are clear about their purpose and perspective from the beginning, New Testament documents from the second generation demonstrate that those in places like Corinth or Galatia were not initially as certain about change as Paul and these two associates. Within a world that appreciated a collectivistic view of persons, innovation or change was not readily accepted. It brought the potential for chaos and uncertainty to a world so appreciative of the status quo. Indeed, the need to protect these groups that were entered at birth typically resulted in great concern for the stranger or one from another group. So persons like Paul and others who were both on the move and on the move because of a recent transition from their own birth-given groups were faced with significant challenges.

Travel in the ancient world was not easy. The Roman (ultimately military) concern with building and maintaining roads helped. But, minimally, one like Paul had to negotiate the physical challenges of sailing, walking, sleeping, and finding food and temporary shelter from the elements. One also had to be constantly aware of "robbers" (Luke 10:29-37). Even with these issues successfully negotiated, Paul and other associates like Titus still had to consider the social concerns created as they were initially perceived more as strangers than as ones from within the group. This process of receiving persons is known as hospitality.[7] Essentially, hospitality in honor-based collectivistic cultures was an extended process that allowed for a stranger to be transformed first to guest and then, potentially, from guest to friend—or enemy. In today's world, hospitality is often associated with entertaining friends, that is, those already recognized as nonstrangers. But in a world where group boundaries were so much more obvious and nonporous, bringing one in or letting one leave required attention.[8] As always, the concern of the group was foremost to avoid shame and sustain honor.

The process of hospitality involved three successive stages. The first step was to test the stranger to see if one from the outside posed any threat to the group. With so much perceived to be at stake, receiving an outsider required an evaluation stage where he (or, in rare instances, she) was assessed as capable of respecting the host group. Initially a patron might take one in through some kind of association (similar job, position in respective society, a previous connection with one from the patron's extended family). Paul holds a number of associations that may have provided him with an initial in. He might have made contacts through his work or trade (1 Cor 4:12; 1 Thess 2:9; Acts fills in these general references to work with information about Paul working with leather, 18:3), his roots in the Pharisee tradition, his extended family (Acts 23:16 references Paul's sister and specifically her son living in Jerusalem), or even through more general ties to others who recognized themselves as "Israel." The necessity to yet "test" these ties or, in honor terms, to get to a point where these ties could be publicly acknowledged was still necessary and important. These tests lie behind Paul's reports of his visits to Jerusalem (Gal 2:1f.) and can also be seen in Paul's concern with sending associates like Titus with letters of recommendation (Rom 16:1; 1 Cor 16:3; 2 Cor 8:16-24) that serve as a bit of an introduction. For collectivistic persons such letters would have served as Paul's testimony that the one who held them (Titus) behaved like Paul and held the same values as Paul. Thus, a host could bring in Titus as if he was Paul. But even with such letters, there was still testing to be done to see if those who held the letters were worthy of them.

In a world where few non-Romans were aware of "rights," the passing of the initial scrutiny only led to a second phase where the larger group observed the guest to see if the guest was capable of respecting the host group's values. Foremost, the patron or host who would ultimately house and feed the stranger en route to friend (relating to the group) or enemy (not related to the group) would evaluate the guest. While under the care of the host, it was important for the guest not to offend the host or arrogantly act as if already a friend. Neither could the guest act as if not under the protection or guidance of the host by refusing the host's guidance or even what the host offered. This second stage was also complicated by the fact that since the guest was somewhat in, any unnecessary dishonoring of the guest would, by association, be perceived as a shaming of the group from which the guest came. So, it was also important for the host not to offend the guest or allow anyone from the host's group to offend the guest. This mutual concern of the guest and host to act appropriately toward one another will be seen in Paul's report of Titus' visit to Corinth (chap. 4).

Finally, having passed one another's respective tests, the third and final step was the public proclamation of guest as "in" (friend) or "out" (enemy). As friend, the guest would leave and praise (honor) the hospitality of his host. Paul's letters indicate he was very keen on spreading such information to the wider network of groups in Christ (Rom 1:8-9; Phil 1:3-5; 1 Thess 1:2-10). Paul also reports to the Corinthians that Titus had reported the appropriate hospitality provided by the Corinthians (see below, chap. 4). At such points, all are friends or, as is more often the case in the second-generation letters, "fictive kin" (brothers, sisters). Of course, the Bible also notes situations where the host does not receive the guest. When the process failed, persons were objectified as simply nonhuman. Without the status of a group host, such objectification could leave one like Paul beaten or otherwise abused—as Paul reports (e.g., 2 Cor 11:23). The so-called passion narratives of the third-generation gospels of Mark and Matthew generally portray Jesus as one without a group (recall Peter's denial) and only a heavenly patron. As such, Jesus is entirely expendable and dies the most heinous death. This breakdown and the subsequent split between ingroups (who walk in light) and enemy (who walk in the darkness of the world) is a fundamental theme throughout the Gospel of John as Jesus, a.k.a. the Word, is not received by the world.

Honorable Change: An Honorable Response to God

Change within a collectivistic culture was a serious matter that could be associated with the shameful estrangement from one's primary groups. So, as Paul and others like Titus promote change, it would have been absolutely necessary for such persons to be able to justify the change. While there is very little suggesting how Titus came to Paul's network, the second-generation letters do include sections where Paul offers his own experience as a paradigm or example for how others in Christ could better transition from past groups to the new. Paul's description of his life in his letter to the Philippians, for example, is to serve as a collectivistic model for those in Philippi who were to be "imitating" Paul and others (Phil 3:17). Analysis of this description will also serve as an example for how one might unpack an ancient high-context communication.

Paul tells the Philippians that prior to promoting God's gospel his life was similar to that of others born in proximity to Palestine. He was "circumcised on the eighth day, of the people of Israel, of the tribe of Benjamin, a Hebrew born of Hebrews; as to the law a Pharisee, as to zeal a persecutor of the church, as to righteousness under the law blameless" (Phil 3:5-6). Up to and including his description of himself as "a Hebrew born of Hebrews," the information describes those groups Paul inherited through birth. The language is compact and may appear to be full of synonyms. But within this characterization of honorable "unoriginality," Paul's initial readers would have picked up on certain nuances that at first might seem unimportant or redundant today. For example, Paul twice moves from a specific to a general qualification or classification. He begins his report with mention of facts about his circumcision and only then reports that he is from the (more general) "people of Israel." This is followed by the classification pair that describes him first as one from the tribe of Benjamin (specific) and then as a member of the more general "Hebrews." That is, he describes himself both as a member of a particular clan (Benjamin) and as a member of a collective of clans descending from God's promise to Abraham. As these clans or tribes centuries ago had became dispersed as punishment for their collective abuse of God's graciousness, Paul was now aware of and specifically interested in telling others how these groups could be together again. The simple answer was that God had now come to allow it. But the difficulty seemingly remained for how to let the presumptions of any one tribe or clan—especially those that remained closely tied to Jerusalem—be just that and not necessary for identity in Christ. At the same time, Paul is admitting his connection to a kind of bloodline begun in Abraham and sustained through Jacob. This bloodline was exclusive. It was not everyone's; it belonged only to Israelites. There is little in the second-generation letters that substantiates the notion that Paul thought God's innovation was for all people. That is not to say that Paul would have opposed non-Israelites joining those in Christ. It is merely to point out that a majority of non-Israelites would not have been interested in what the Israelite God was up to now or in the past. By contrast, later generations would bend this view (see above, chap. 1 about the fourth-generation).

By indicating he was circumcised on the eighth day, Paul informs his audience that he was a Hebrew (of the line of Benjamin) born in an area—or at least within an extended family—where a ritual like circumcision was appreciated and thus common.[9] In some of the later Maccabean literature of the second century BC, (literature not recognized as canonical by later Protestant groups) circumcision becomes a mark signifying a kind of blood brotherhood for those interested in keeping the newly reconstituted Judea from any outside influence of empire (1 Macc 1:11-15, 48-50; 2:46). In Paul's day, circumcision was still probably viewed as a normative behavior within this limited regional area. By contrast it would not be a defining mark for all Diaspora Israelites. Writing to the Philippians who lived over one thousand miles from Jerusalem, Paul does not pause to explain what such a ritual does for one on the eighth day. Nor does Paul indicate that such a ritual would have been appreciated by the recipients of the letter. Paul merely mentions it as a way of noting the difference between his past behaviors and his current life now concerned with the Philippians. Like these Philippians, he believes himself to be an Israelite. But as a group interested in responding authentically to the newness of what God had done, Paul does not see such past behavior as anything important. As he would state elsewhere, neither circumcision nor noncircumcision are anything (Gal 5:6; 6:15; Rom 2–4). Some contemporary textbooks suggest circumcision was one of the final lines one would cross in the transformation from some other group to Israel (or, as many texts describe such persons, a "Jew"). But for most, being "in Israel" was something that happened at birth. There are other contexts where various actions and behaviors are noted as having been considered by others (outsiders or insiders) as acting *like* an Israelite.[10] To act like an Israelite and to have been born into Israel, however, were always two potentially distinguishable matters.

As Paul continues with his description, he notes his previous association with a party known as the Pharisees. This statement is especially loaded or high context in that it distinguishes him from the group known as Sadducees. The Sadducees apparently recognized fewer books as part of their Scripture and held different notions about how to interpret them. As a Pharisee, Paul would have held very specific notions about how to live appropriately under God. First and foremost, Pharisees assumed that God wanted all Israelites to live with an appreciation of exclusivity, of being set apart by and for God. This unique status in the world would allow others to appreciate the Pharisaic notion of one supreme God who was yet opposed by an evil or other power. Paul would have appreciated the Pharisaic notion of a kingdom to come where a messiah or savior would bring an end to the world as it was known. He would have appreciated that those who oppose God and God's desire for human life would be judged and subsequently annihilated leaving only the righteous to live with God in a kind of paradise like the Garden of Eden.[11]

After his statement about being a Hebrew among Hebrews, Paul makes slightly different types of claims. He is no longer speaking about groups into which he was born, but his level of commitment to such groups. Specifically Paul notes he was "as to zeal a persecutor of the Church." Just as Paul's claim to have "fear of the Lord" (2 Cor 5:11; cf. Ps 1:1) doesn't quite convey an emotional state of being scared so much as having reverence for another, the term "zeal" doesn't quite convey the notion that Paul was a vibrant personality or one full of cheerful energy. In Paul's day the underlying Greek term was used to express one's commitment. Here, Paul uses zeal to express his commitment to his former group.[12] Again, within a collectivistic culture, commitment to the group is a virtue. The acts of persecution then complement the self-proclaimed zeal by way of example. It might sound strange to contemporary readers, but these acts of persecution were a kind of spirituality in the sense that they were a way of living out his values, values the collectivistic Paul held as a member of a group. In other words, Paul is stating that he was so committed to his Pharisee view of a world that had been revealed by God that he was willing to persecute anyone who wasn't honorably acting as if in the same group. To belabor the obvious, he certainly wasn't persecuting Romans. In fact, from the Roman view, such inner Israelite squabbles often seemed worth little more than the amusement portrayed by the guards at the crucifixion of Jesus (Luke 23:36-38). Paul's concerns were with other Israelites, sons of Abraham, who, in following their perception of new things God had done in bringing Jesus back from death, had veered from the status quo perceived by other Israelites.

Paul's report of being blameless is similarly concerned with expressing his zeal for his former group. As an ingroup designation, Paul is telling the Philippians that no one from his former Israelite group was able to dishonor him publicly for any failure to behave as expected. Presumably, the groups he was persecuting would have found plenty about him worthy of blame. At the same time, of course, other groups like the Sadducees would have found him at least somewhat worthy of correction. But as "outsiders," their relatively differing opinions would have been both expected and ultimately less important than the appreciation shown by other Pharisees.

Once this high-context literature is unpacked a bit, Paul's description of his past suggests that as an honorable member of his former groups, he had *not* been looking for change. Yet, change happened. In his collectivistic world, the process of how this change came about would have been of great interest to others concerned with the integrity of someone who could abandon a group to which he had been so zealous or committed. In a world of personal causality, change is always ascribed to a someone. For Paul, that being was God. As Paul tells it, God appeared to him. And although this personal cause needed to be articulated, the appearance itself likely didn't create suspicion for those who initially heard about it. References to such contacts with the nonhuman world are found throughout the New Testament.[13] The third-generation gospels describe Jesus as having such an experience at his baptism and shortly thereafter as he is tested in the nonhuman wilderness (Mark 1:12-13; Matt 4:1-11). These documents also describe all or some of the disciples having had such experiences both before the crucifixion (Jesus walking on the water, Mark 6:45-52; Matt 14:22-33; John 6:15-21 and Jesus being transfigured, Mark 9:2-8; Matt 17:1-8) and after (Matt 28:9-10; John 20:19-29). The fourth-generation Acts of the Apostles has dozens of descriptions of humans experiencing various manifestations of the divine world. These include visions, manifestations of the spirit that include speech and healings, insights into activities, and trances.[14] Though not as pervasive, these encounters with the nonhuman world are also found throughout second-generation letters. Many within these groups are reminded of their experience of the effects of this risen Jesus in their new lives in Christ. Fewer have had more direct experiences with the divine world (e.g., 2 Cor 12:2-4).

The fact that such visions, revelations, or other forms of non-human contact are so prevalent in the Bible can create tensions for some modern readers. As noted in a previous study in this series, contemporary individualist cultures are aware of such extraordinary experiences. We recognize a variety of alternate states of consciousness. But, in general, most North Americans are not as comfortable as the ancients when it comes to recognizing such nonregular experiences as legitimate or thus meaningful enough to write about for others.[15] A contemporary individualist might be more inclined to speak about an individual's perceived experience along with his or her ability to process such events in a way that "reasonably" relates these experiences to other events. Further, while no single event would likely be credited for moving most Americans in a radically different direction, one might welcome such an event as a proverbial "last straw" en route to a cumulative effect leading to some aspect of change. The point is that we portray ourselves as in control of the process. We "decide" to change.[16]

In contrast, Paul's descriptions of such encounters with the divine portray him as passive. They are specifically noted as responsible both for his actions (his second trip to Jerusalem, Gal 2:2) and his understanding of certain suffering (2 Cor 12:8-9). Most important, such encounters are responsible for his present role as an apostle/agent. Paul's description of this event is found in a few documents. It is referred to in Galatians (see below chap. 3). But this initial vision is perhaps most fully described in 1 Corinthians 15:1-11. The more immediate context is a concern with the Corinthian misunderstanding of the innovation given by Paul. As the constant change agent, Paul seeks to sustain the group through this misunderstanding by addressing the particular Corinthian reinvention of the resurrection. As he prepares to argue against the misunderstanding and for the correct understanding (1 Cor 15:12-28), Paul describes visions of the resurrection. The raised Jesus "appeared to Cephas [Peter's Judean, or non-Hellenized, name], then the twelve" (15:5). Then, at once, the raised Jesus appeared to a group of more than five hundred. Here Paul notes most of these are still alive though some have died (15:6). Then he appeared to James and then to all the apostles (15:7). Finally he appeared to Paul. Paul states, "Last of all, as to one untimely born, he appeared to me also" (15:8). Like a Joseph or David or any person God chooses despite their having been last in line according to the conventions of their day, God appeared to Paul. Paul goes on to qualify the vision as something that happened in spite of his persecution of groups called by God. He also notes that since his vision he has "worked harder than any of those" aforementioned. But, like visions, the ability to get things done in a world of personal causality must ultimately be attributed to a someone. So, Paul further qualifies his efforts or work as God's "grace" (gift) working through him (1 Cor 15:10).

Paul's initial experience of the divine was not that of the Bible's more typical holy man.[17] The occasional explicit mention of his experience of the nonhuman world (noted above, Gal 1:1, 2:2, etc.) or this more profound vision of the raised Jesus should not be too far removed from other less personalized experiences. Rather than the visions per se, the second-generation letters are far more likely to note the God-given gifts or grace manifested within the groups as a whole (e.g., 1 Cor 12–14). Paul never lists these gifts for the sake of listing them. He is more concerned about having groups (like the Corinthians) realize that such manifestations are ultimately nothing if they are not recognized as coming from God and applied to the service of one another.

As his visions are mentioned, they serve his honor. At the same time, the comparatively fewer cited occasions of contact with the divine world need not leave one with the impression that Paul experienced them less than others (e.g., those portrayed in Acts). As Paul indicates throughout his letters, he is so entwined with the divine that his body seems to be the only obvious thing keeping him from the fuller and more permanent vision of heaven he anticipates (Phil 3:10-12). Like others who experience similar encounters, Paul sees his experience as ultimately for others and to the benefit of others.

At the same time, Paul's characterization of being the last to have the risen Jesus revealed to him gives him a unique role.

This role is very much Paul's focus in his letter to the Galatians, discussed in the next chapter. For now it is important to recognize that the same God credited as providing him with a vision of the raised Jesus is credited in the letter to the Galatians as responsible for commissioning Paul as one sent (an apostle) to the Israelites dispersed throughout the nations. Given the above distinctions characterizing the differences between the second and third generations, it is important to note that the heavenly commissioner depicted in the letter to the Galatians is not the earthly Jesus, but the resurrected Christ. By distinction, the fourth-generation book of Acts fills out such encounters between Paul and the divine through three expanded versions (Acts 9; 22; 26).[18]

The context assumed by second-generation persons is quite distinct from our contemporary world. The appreciation for what a first-century person like Paul or Titus valued or how such persons perceived their world will help us understand how one like Titus functioned in his respective associations with Corinth or Galatia. As the next chapters assess more specific data about Paul and Titus, these insights will be assumed and occasionally recalled.

CHAPTER 3

Titus According to the Data from the Letter to the Galatians

Paul wrote his letter to the Galatians aware that others had come to Galatia demanding certain behaviors Paul and others like Titus considered irrelevant given what God was now doing. Much of the information in the first chapters of the letter to the Galatians appears to be autobiographical. Unlike modern autobiographical essays, however, Paul is writing specifically to demonstrate his honor.[1] Aware that his gospel is tied directly to his character as the agent of that message, Paul writes to assure the Galatians that their connection to him and his gospel is honorable and need not be modified to include behaviors suggested by others.

There is only a brief mention of Titus in the letter to the Galatians. Paul remembers him as a companion in one of two trips made to Jerusalem. Yet, in this collectivistic world, both the broader form of writing within which Titus is referenced and the specific words Paul chose to describe him say much about who Titus was and why Paul mentioned him in this particular letter. As noted in the previous chapter, one's identity in a collectivistic culture could be sufficiently known with consideration of those with whom one associated. So, it was more than insignificant small talk when one heard of adjectives describing a "Jesus of Nazareth" or a "Galilean" like Peter. As such, it was important for Paul to present Titus as both worthy of Paul's company and, by extension, one whose exemplary behavior in Jerusalem should be modeled by those in Galatia. By contrast, the letter claims others mentioned do not share the same honor as Paul and Titus. Their vacillating behavior is offered as a contrast to the more honorable life demonstrated by Titus and Paul. Following a brief overview of the context for the letter and some of its key features, the remainder of this chapter will focus on unpacking the role of Titus and Paul as presented to the Galatians.

Overview of Galatians

Paul's initial contact with the Galatians appears to have been an unplanned event.[2] His letter reminds them that "it was because of a bodily ailment that I preached the gospel to you at first" (4:13). In Paul's world of personal causality, of course, an illness or physical infirmity was not the result of a something (e.g., stress causing a higher blood pressure, genetics, a virus, bacteria, or other things discovered only in the last centuries). So even if Paul had initially intended only to pass through the area en route to some farther western location like Ephesus, Paul would have come to understand his experience in Galatia as the result of *the* ultimate personal causality, God. God was to be publicly praised for providing Paul the opportunity to bring news of God's innovation to Galatia (1:1-5), just as God was to be praised as working through those who treated Paul as if he were an "angel of God" (an intermediary between humans and God), as if he were Jesus the Messiah (4:14).

The letter provides no insight into how long Paul was ill or how long he remained in Galatia after his illness. Nor is it exactly clear how long Paul had been away from those now challenged in his absence. Most contemporary commentaries place the date for Paul's letter to the Galatians in the mid-50s, about twenty years after the death and resurrection of Jesus. So, one might suggest Paul's amazement over how "quickly" the Galatians were experiencing problems (1:6) indicates that a previous (if not initial) contact had been within the past year or so (ca. 53–54).

While the Corinthian correspondence mentions both letters (1 Cor 5:9; 7:1) and personal reports (1 Cor 1:11) used to communicate problems or concerns to Paul, there is nothing in Galatians to explain how Paul became aware of problems developing there. As a change agent concerned with the continued reception of the innovation, Paul would have made every effort to sustain the communication necessary to move any newly formed group beyond problems that would jeopardize its integrity. Empathetic with the concerns raised by the storming going on in Galatia, Paul characterizes his efforts with the Galatians as, again, painfully giving birth until Christ is "formed" (passive, personal causality) within them (Gal 4:19).

Some comment that the letter appears to display Paul's anger or elevated emotion. Paul may or may not have been emotional when writing this letter. In a collectivistic culture always concerned with the social or public face, the letter was less intended to unveil Paul's inner feelings or emotions and more likely to further Paul's call to return the Galatians back to their earlier reception of the innovation. In some instances the letter is less than typical. For example, it lacks the section where Paul typically praised the manifestations of God's gifts within the group. Yet, Paul's efforts here are like those in any letter from him and his associates, designed to demonstrate care and concern for the group's continued existence "in Christ." One can see his concern with this embeddedness when he addresses the Galatians with the fictive kin term "brothers" (NRSV, 3:15; 4:12, 28; 6:1, 18). For Paul, the groups brought together in Christ were to relate to one another because God was the father, patron, or provider making it possible for all Israelites in Galatia and elsewhere to exist. As a collectivistic person, Paul's use of such fictive kin terms was a way to remind the Galatians that the values and norms held by "our" fictive family were to be at the forefront of concern whenever possible and certainly whenever challenged by others from beyond the group.

In addition to calling them brothers, Paul does not hesitate to call them bewitched and foolish (3:1). A change agent in the United States could seldom expect to be effective in bringing a group to change while calling some or all bewitched or foolish. Paul, however, need not be understood here as communicating any angry, emotional jabs intended to reveal his inner feelings about those in Galatia. Nor is it presumed that Paul is fickle and had suddenly changed his mind about those otherwise referred to as brothers. Rather, these terms were used as a way of motivating the Galatians to return to a full appreciation of the need to sustain integrity within the groups founded by God and through Paul and others. For Paul and his collectivistic associates, a fool was not someone incapable of doing complex computations or thinking creatively. A fool was essentially someone who didn't know who or how. Like honor, ancient wisdom was tied to one's ability to know "who" was important and "how" to adapt their behaviors and customs in order to interact with them appropriately. A wise person both knew and praised the benefactors of one's group. A wise person knew who was in that group and the behaviors and values that would have been expected from those within the group. Those who didn't "know who," those who didn't appreciate and respond to the behaviors and values of the group were to be dishonored. And anyone who took seriously one without honor would be a fool. In this context, Paul's charge that the Galatians were foolish was far from being mean for the sake of being mean. It was a kind of call to own up to and, more specifically, to act in accordance with one's collectivistic identity. Paul's words would have appealed to the Galatians' sensitivity to protect the honor of their status, to consider themselves as a group that should have recognized and displayed the behaviors and values held by the larger group of those in Christ. As Paul understood it then, the situation for the Galatians was this: either they were going to continue to associate with the others who came to the Galatians with concerns about adapting certain behaviors, or they were going to rebuke this outside influence and sustain the insights brought by Paul and lived out by Greek Israelites elsewhere who lived in Christ. If they went the former route and did not share integrity with Paul's broader network in Christ, they were at risk of losing their integrity as a group. Consequently, Paul's work, all that Paul had declared possible in Christ, would have to be judged as wasted (4:11). But as the consummate change agent, Paul was not ready to anticipate such a shameful ending. With his hope of avoiding discontinuity, he writes that he is confident they "will take no other view than mine" (Gal 5:10).

Like Paul, those creating a crisis for the Galatians are tied to a gospel. Of course, in Paul's view there really was no other gospel. Yet, the Galatians' perception of one requires Paul to qualify it as "*contrary* to that which" they "received" from Paul (Gal 1:9; emphasis added). It was, by extension, other than the gospel of divine origin. The contents of this other gospel are not clear. But Paul's response suggests the other gospel differed especially in its interest to have the Galatians adapt provincial behaviors typically associated with Judeans. In particular, the letter mentions meal customs (2:11-14), attention to certain unique calendar observations (4:10), and a repeated concern with circumcision (2:4-10; 6:15; etc.) that are associated with a life lived in the "flesh" (Gal 3:3; 4:29; 5:13-24; 6:8-13). Paul and those with him are not interested in a life in the flesh. They are not interested in adapting or sustaining Judean meal customs, calendar concerns, or circumcision. The awareness of what God was doing new through Jesus had made these formerly appropriate behaviors obsolete. At the same time, neither was the suspension of these customs mandatory (Gal 5:6).

Most English translations depict the Galatians as "turning" from Paul and the gospel (1:6). Aware of the fundamental notion that change is due to someone, however, it is possible to translate the underlying Greek as a passive. Conceptually, Paul would have been noting the Galatians "had been turned."[3] Those responsible for the turning are never given names, but they are characterized both explicitly and more subtly. Paul's more explicit characterizations begin with the charge that these outsiders wanted to confuse the Galatians and pervert the gospel of Christ (1:7). The underlying Greek terms generally had to do with the corruption or change of identity. As shown above, Paul took considerable effort to justify his move from Pharisee to agent or apostle of God's new activity. By contrast, the charge here suggests those bringing the other gospel were persons interested in change for the sake of instability. In the political context of Paul's day, the effort to confuse and pervert were associated with the language of insurrection, that is, behavior that does not sustain the integrity of the group.[4] Again, in collectivistic cultures, this would be a charge leveled against the lowest type of persons. Further contrasted to Paul's desire to bring Christ fulfilled, Paul characterizes the outsiders' interest in circumcision as a matter only serving their own (outsider) status (6:13). At a time when circumcision probably involved only a small incision, an act sufficient for the production of blood, Paul provides the Galatians with a provocative thought for these outsiders who promote it for their own gain. Paul wished those upsetting the Galatians would "mutilate themselves!" (Gal 5:12; the NAB and NRSV have "castrate themselves"). Of course, such an act would, rather ironically, make circumcision moot. Second, as eunuchs, these men would be incapable of producing a further generation of Israelites presumably needing to be circumcised. Third, such an act would bring social shame from those Judean associates who would no longer be able to recognize such males as worthy of a place in "the assembly of the LORD" (Deut 23:1) or Israel.

Titus in Galatians

The specific function of Titus unfolds within the letter's first two chapters. While he does not appear by name until the second chapter, his role as a companion of Paul is set up by material included in the first chapter. As a unit, the two chapters serve as an encomium, a particular rhetorical form within which one told of one's honorable life.[5] As described in a number of ancient rhetorical handbooks, an encomium is a kind of praise of one's status or a claim to honor. Essentially, Paul utilizes this section at the beginning of his letter to ask the Galatians to recall that he and his God-given gospel are more honorable than the gospel brought in by others. A part of that honor is his relationship with Titus. The encomium begins (1:11) and ends (2:21) with reference to the meaning of Jesus being raised. Within this narrative frame, Paul relates his memory of several events that portray his honorable response to this foundational event. Following his opening statement (1:11-12), Paul presents favorable attributes of his collectivistic life (1:13–2:10). These can be divided into a characterization of his former life (1:13-14), a justification for his being moved from that life (1:15-17), and a characterization of his honorable new life (1:18–2:10). Last, Paul compares himself to others (2:11-21).

Paul opened his letter clearly marking himself as an "apostle" (1:1), that is, one sent to perform a task. Having never met Jesus or spent time traveling with him, Paul never makes any claim to be a disciple, that is, one who studied with Jesus the teacher. Paul is also very quick to relate the agent or source of his role as apostle. This is initially defined negatively (not by humans) and, second, through God, the one who raised Jesus from the dead (1:1). Following his wishes of divine grace and peace (1:3-5) and an initial overview of what he perceives to be quickly developing problems in Galatia (1:6-10), Paul further defines the gospel he proclaimed. Negatively, it was not human either as taught or conveyed by a human (1:11-12a). To the contrary, it was a gospel received as a revelation of Jesus (raised) the Christ (1:12). Two issues related to Paul's honor were here communicated. On the one hand, Paul was reminding his audience of his status as one divinely chosen. Paul's experience of the revelation made that clear. On the other hand, Paul is also noting a kind of justification for his lack of attention to information about the earthly life and times of Jesus from Galilee. Jesus was not recognized as the Christ because of his birth and early life as a Galilean Israelite. His place in God's heaven is only because of God's resurrection.

For some modern readers, such a statement makes little sense. Yet, it is only following the fourth-century creed created by bishops gathered to articulate the newly emerging Roman-sponsored Christianity that people will confess their understanding of a triune God. And in that creed the English states one "person" of this Trinity "rose" from the dead on the third day. Within the creed, the force, source, or personal causality of that rising can be rather ambiguous. The second- and third-generation documents most often portray Jesus as having been (passive) raised. In context, the source of that rising (event) is none other than God, the ultimate personal causality.

Paul next provides his encomium with a select characterization of both his pre-vision life as a Pharisee and his post-vision life as an apostle. He does not contribute the detail we might expect in a modern autobiography. He is, however, focused on presenting himself as one who was consistently loyal to or embedded in respective groups. Just as he had been loyal to the Pharisee group into which he had been born, he is now loyal to the groups he helped to establish in Christ. As in his letter to the Philippians (discussed above), Paul here notes he once sought out those who turned from Judean conventions in order to destroy them (1:13). He once lived exceedingly committed ("zealous") to upholding the Judean customs (1:14). As one guided by these customs, Paul sought out those who had abandoned them as a way of honoring both the God who revealed them and those like himself who received them. In the Philippians account, Paul parlays this description of his past to an anticipation of a different, but not yet completed life in Christ. By distinction, Paul's emphasis in Galatians is the timing of the change: "But *when* he who had set me apart before I was born . . . was pleased to reveal his son to me" (1:15-16a; emphasis added). Paul's change is portrayed as something initiated in the womb but as something that was to be manifested after living for a time as a Pharisee. In other words, Paul had not always been aware of what new things God was doing. Yet, from his current perspective, he knows he is one like Jacob (later named Israel), Isaiah, Jeremiah, or others described in Scripture as having been removed from their status quo lifestyle to serve God differently only later in life.⁶ Paul suggests God authored lives like these to be lived out for a time according to the conventions of their birth. Then, with God's revelation, God would call or reassign (and, in some instances rename) them to announce God's new actions. It might also be worth noting that these actions announced to Jeremiah and others like Paul were radically different from the status quo and, as such, not immediately received by most.

With past and present honorably characterized as divinely authored, Paul articulates his current role as one who received a revelation "in order that I might preach him [Jesus Christ] among the Gentiles [nations]" (1:16a), that is, to those Israelites who had been living well beyond Palestine. Still focused on his honor, Paul now shifts to describe his response to the revelation. As divinely called, his first response was not to seek human approval (1:16b). Stated first in the negative, Paul notes his response was not to go up to Jerusalem to those already apostles (1:17a). Instead he went to "Arabia" (1:17b). Paul's high-context letter provides no explanation of his purpose there or activity. Nor does he provide detail about where he was in Arabia. Many recent commentaries understand this time in Arabia as a kind of initial run. Therein Paul is tied to initial work in the Nabataean Empire.⁷ It may be, however, that Paul is telling the Galatians of his time spent within the wide-open spaces unmanaged by the human realm. Similar to the later third-generation characterization of a recently baptized Jesus made aware of a new role and subsequently tested in the desert (Mark 1:9-13), Paul may be simply stating that nothing from such encounters with the spirit world led him to any different conclusions about the new direction he had been given. At any rate, he closes the section with the report that he had "returned to Damascus" (1:17c). Perhaps he was ready for a second try. Perhaps he was indicating that he was now sure he was ready to begin.

Following this rationale for his transformation from Pharisee to agent or apostle, the collectivistic Paul next describes two trips to Jerusalem. Essentially, he relates to the Galatians his interest in having his reception of the gospel recognized by others like him. While the descriptions of these two trips seem to leave out a good deal of information, the details that are included indicate Paul's sustained concern with demonstrating his honor. In his 1 Corinthians report of the risen Christ, Paul stated that Jesus last appeared to him, but had first appeared to Cephas, Peter's non-Greek, or native Aramaic, name. This is precisely the man Paul reports visiting in Jerusalem. As noted in the previous chapter, traveling from one place to another was not a simple task. It required a great deal of effort to sustain both physical health and social standing. Although the data provided is minimal, Paul's description of this visit is consistent with concerns for hospitality. Given Paul's past as a Pharisee and the relatively recent move to a life in Christ, it is probable that anyone who would have received him in Jerusalem would have been subject to concern from at least two groups. The Israelite Pharisees (and other Jerusalem-based parties like the Sadducees) would have found Paul a fool for having abandoned the temple-mediated system into which he was born. On the other hand, those in Jerusalem who now lived aware that God had raised Jesus, those whom Paul had formerly persecuted, might have found his new life relatively untested. With such circumstances in mind, Paul tells the Galatians that his first trip to Jerusalem brought him to stay only with Cephas. Beyond that, Paul only notes the duration of his visit, fifteen days (1:18).[8] Paul does not inform the Galatians about what the two did or where they may have roamed. But, given the model of hospitality, one might understand Paul communicating to the Galatians that he had been in Jerusalem with Cephas long enough to have made the transition from guest to friend. Whatever they did and wherever it was done, Paul had acted appropriately as a guest taken in by the patron Cephas. Another matter Paul related about this first visit to Jerusalem is that he had seen only one other, James, the brother of the Lord.[9] This is followed by an oath where God is called to serve as Paul's witness (1:20). The oath indicates that the matter is serious. Yet, exactly what is serious (was it specifically James or was it the number of persons with whom he came into contact?) is not spelled out in detail.

Following this first trip, Paul reports he traveled to Syria and Cilicia. Again, he provides no details, but given his tendency to encounter larger concentrations of people, he may have worked in places like Antioch, Pamphilia, and Psidia. Following this apparent aside about travels after his stay in Jerusalem, Paul returns the focus to those in Jerusalem. He tells the Galatians that throughout this time he remained largely unknown in and around Jerusalem. They had only heard things about him. And when they did, they "glorified God" because the one who had been persecuting was now proclaiming "the faith" (1:22-24). As is his tendency, Paul is never long without noting personal causality. As a whole, the report of the first trip to Jerusalem suggests Paul's concern was to communicate to the Galatians his sensitivity for his host. In particular, his concern was to communicate the trip's privacy.

Paul next reports his second trip to Jerusalem. This occurred more than a decade after the first trip. It differed from the previous trip in that this second trip was motivated by a revelation from God. Further, this second trip was made in the company of Barnabas and Titus (2:1).[10] The concern with privacy only alluded to above is here more explicitly stated. Paul notes that the purpose of the trip was to lay out in private before the Jerusalem pillars the gospel he presents to the Greek (non-Judean) Israelites (the *ethne*; 2:2). Paul knows his gospel is from God. But, as he presents it, God had now determined it was time to have some of those in Jerusalem recognize that Paul was not now running, nor had he run, "in vain" (2:2).[11] As a result of the trip, both Paul's group and the group embedded in the pillars mutually recognize Paul's station in life or honor. While the formal use of encomium in the letter suggests the Galatians should judge Paul as honorable, the element of comparison also allows for others besides Paul to be judged.

Paul's mention of Barnabas is only clear later in the letter. Titus, however, is immediately qualified as one "not compelled to be circumcised, though he was a Greek" (2:3). The term translated as "compelled" can more literally convey a notion of one being forced to follow a certain course or "to act in a particular manner."[12] As Paul's recollections of events in Jerusalem unfold, it is clear that some in Jerusalem had expected Titus to receive circumcision or change his course, manner, or behavior (Gal 2:4). It is also clear from the letter that Paul's mention of Titus as a Greek is synonymous with—among other things—noting he had not been circumcised (Gal 2:7-9). Third-generation gospels can give the modern reader the impression that a key distinction among Israelites was made between Sadducee and Pharisee. That was true, perhaps especially in and around Jerusalem. From Paul's more widely Mediterranean perspective, however, a more important distinction among Israelites was made between Judeans and those Israelites Paul calls Greeks, that is, the residents of the Hellenistic cities Paul addressed. Such cities sometimes held ethnic quarters where Paul's "Greek" Israelite brothers and sisters lived in Christ.

In a collectivistic culture, calling someone a "Greek" or "circumcised" (or, for that matter, following a certain calendar or identifying with a certain figure like Abraham, etc.) would have stereotypically defined the person as a member of a particular group. Like Israelites, Greeks could have been a homogenous group to non-Greek "outsiders." At one level such people could have been perceived as generally sharing many cultural markers. If necessary or desired, however, Greeks could be further differentiated by labels associating them with more distinct local and often ethnic names: Macedonians, Athenians, etc. Labeling someone a "Greek" in a letter to other Israelites who would have considered themselves Greeks was a way to both relate and rate Titus as one of the received culture, one of "us." By contrast, non-Greeks would have been those perceived as "other," if not as those from a less refined culture. For example, most Greeks appear to have found the Judean ritual of circumcision rather barbaric and thus something shameful for any "Greek" to adapt. At the same time, of course, the Judean perspective would have been that their own cultural behaviors were superior to those of the sinful Greeks (Gal 2:15), Israelites who failed to do what the ingroup Judeans did, that is, honor the Judean God by following what were perceived to be divinely revealed customs. That is precisely why before his vision of the raised Jesus, Paul had persecuted those who responded to and trusted in God's action of raising Jesus from death. These persons were not behaving consistently with those who respected all of the more conventional Judean markers of identity.

As Paul's account of his second trip to Jerusalem continues, he is clear to note that the distinctions held by either group (Greeks and Judeans) were not of the utmost importance. Paul is also careful to indicate to the Galatians that he had been willing and capable of clarifying these distinctions in private with the pillars. As an honorable person, Paul did not enter Jerusalem a second time with Titus in tow hoping to create either conflict or tension for the one who hosted his first trip. Yet, despite his efforts, Paul reports the trip turned into a matter for larger social consumption and judgment when "false brethren" secretly arrived "to spy out our freedoms" and sought to bring an end to those freedoms (2:4). Initially, these false brothers are not at all associated "with" the pillars, the group defined as James, Cephas, and John. So, when Paul subsequently reports "we" did not submit to them (2:5), he probably has in mind not only Titus and Barnabas, but also this group of three, the highly respected pillars within Jerusalem. While it doesn't look very democratic from today's perspective, it is possible for contemporary readers to imagine Paul conveying the notion to the Galatians that if the false brothers had not crept in, the whole visit could have ended with a mutual recognition that both the pillars and Paul were involved in respectively honorable pursuits. Neither Paul (and those with him) nor Peter (and those with him) had been running in vain. But spies did enter.

Consistent with other high-context writing, Paul does not record any specific dialogue or even relate many details about how others related to him. He eventually describes how the matter of his visit came to be resolved before a wider audience. Before noting the resolution, however, Paul presents what might appear to be a kind of aside. More likely, it sets up the resolution that follows. Paul wants to make it clear that while he associated with James, Cephas, and John, the pillars (or those honored in

Jerusalem), these persons "added nothing" to him (2:6). A contemporary reader more tuned to current traditions than the context of Paul's day might wonder if such language was disrespectful of Peter. From the second generation's perspective, a perspective created by the God who gave Paul the vision of the raised Jesus, there was no disrespect so much as a reasonable expectation for mutual respect. In Paul's view both Peter (to the circumcised) and Paul (to the uncircumcised) were equally called by God for their respective service (2:7-8). Paul specifically notes the Jerusalem pillars had recognized "the grace that was given to me" (2:9). Within the concept of patronage and honor, this statement relates the public affirmation of Paul's (God-given) claim to honor. Each was mutually recognized to have his own area or boundary and each recognized that the one granting access to the innovation was one and the same patron, God (2:7-8).

Paul's status before those in Jerusalem concluded with a ritualized form of recognition. The recognition is specifically reported to have come from James, Cephas, and John. Again, these three are qualified as the beloved pillars, the respected in Jerusalem. Specifically the rite involved the pillars offering both Paul and Barnabas "the right hand of fellowship" (2:9). While there are differing views of what this handshake implied in its context, it is clear that the prerogative of offering would typically have fallen to those perceived to be in the superior position.[13] In the context of their recently adopted home turf in Jerusalem, such a position would go to the pillars by default. So while some modern commentators are determined to read these meetings in Jerusalem as the context for Paul receiving some sort of commission, Paul makes it clear that, in this case, form does not match substance thoroughly. In the context of his time and place, Paul played by the rules. He accepted the handshake as it had been offered by those who as host would have been expected to offer it. At the same time, however, Paul is clear that these pillars "added nothing" to him. As these events are related to the Galatians, Paul is still depicting himself as an honorable friend, one sensitive to his own status and the status of his host, Cephas.

As a guest, Paul was willing to receive such a handshake even if he had not been seeking it. In fact, he was willing to receive the handshake even if the only ones to receive anything were the pillars who, as Paul tells it, had come to perceive the grace or gift given to Paul (Gal 2:9). As pillars or honored, one could assume that what they received and publicly recognized would have been adapted by those who held them in esteem. Paul's reports of subsequent meetings will suggest that was not entirely the case. At any rate, the events described in the encomium go to Paul's honor as one who was willing to get on with the core issues and leave the pillars with honor before at least most of their own.

Beyond the mutual interest to have it known how each was to work in their respective areas, another mutual concern was the interest to remember the poor. Paul concludes his report of the second trip to Jerusalem by noting he was asked only one thing, that we "remember the poor, which very thing I was eager to do" (Gal 2:10). Paul is still making claims to his honor. Specifically, he is comparing himself positively to the pillars who also hold such interests. Once again, those in Jerusalem had nothing new to add or bring to Paul. He was already willing to manifest whatever it was that the request to "remember" involved.

Although Titus is explicitly mentioned only in 2:1 and then probably last implied in the pronoun "*we* did not yield" (Gal 2:5; emphasis added), he remained a part of Paul's group. Thus, it is important to note that Paul did not describe the handshake of fellowship being offered to Titus. It is only offered to Paul and Barnabas. What impressions or information the Galatians would have gathered from this detail is far from explicit. Given the general trajectory of Paul's report, it would seem likely the pillars were being characterized as concerned with their purity. As uncircumcised, Titus could have been perceived by some as "out of bounds." Paul's subsequent recollection highlights this concern with purity. Paul relates a visit by Cephas to Antioch. Paul is still comparing himself. But here Paul's description of the visit portrays Cephas as one with comparatively less honor. If by offering the handshake of fellowship Cephas and the other pillars had presented themselves as the more honored in Jerusalem, Paul was the better man in Antioch.

Paul makes it clear that he did not initiate the tension or challenge. Cephas condemned himself; "he stood condemned" (2:11). Cephas had acted as a hypocrite or, more literally, an actor, one capable of wearing two faces (2:13). Specifically, Paul notes that before a contingent from James came to Antioch, Cephas (the former Galilean and now Judean) had eaten with those other Israelites with the Greek customs. After this arrival, however, Cephas "drew back" in fear of "the circumcision party" (2:12). Again, the fear was not simply or even primarily an emotional state so much as a note about Cephas' respect or consideration for those from his home turf. Paul further remarks that this initial action by the respected Cephas served as an example prompting other Judeans to do the same (2:13). Paul then notes the cumulative actions cause even Barnabas, the one who came to Jerusalem with Paul and Titus, to follow. Again, it may be that many modern readers who appreciate low-context literature might sense that many details have been left out or ignored. For example, we are given a very sparse dialogue. But in high-context documents like Galatians, the way the people are described as separating probably said enough, particularly about Paul and, by contrast, Barnabas and Cephas.

Given the context of requirements for hospitality, it is likely that, at minimum, all involved would have recognized this was a difficult situation. It was likely realized that while there was a level of commonality in their mutual appreciation for the new things God was doing, there was also some degree of tension created by the recognition of issues that distinguished one group from another. There was a breakdown or a point of distinction to be made between the friends. The guest had not acted totally in compliance with the hosts even after one from within the host community, that is, Paul, had acknowledged that the behavior of Cephas was a matter for concern. While Cephas and the other pillars might have been moved to recognize and publicly portray Paul's agency, at least one of these pillars—Cephas—was far from convinced he could be(come) like Paul. Whatever potential for further fallout this event would have created, it was sufficient for Paul to communicate to the Galatians that the actions of Cephas had caused Barnabas and others to be "carried away" (Gal 2:13). At the same time, the behavior of Cephas and others in Antioch might have led Paul to new insights. Perhaps Paul would consider the consequences of this event in Antioch influential for his further relationships with Cephas, the pillars, and, for that matter, Jerusalem. This recollection would go a long way to justify and demonstrate his generation's lack of concern with those survivors of the first generation. It also could have shaped Paul's concerns as he prepared to organize a gift for the saints in Jerusalem, something the Galatians had been asked to consider (1 Cor 16:1).

Given the earlier distinct perspectives held by each of the various generations of New Testament documents, one might anticipate that the tensions described by Paul were either muted or otherwise altered by the fourth-generation book of Acts. In fact, Titus is never even mentioned in Acts. While Luke presents a situation where circumcision and meal customs were a matter for concern in the early days following the resurrection of Jesus (Acts 15), the depiction given by Luke has no mention of Paul confronting Peter. Nor does any similar scene lead to the falling out of Barnabas, let alone the notion that Barnabas had been led astray. Nor does Paul travel to Jerusalem to engage this matter as a result of any divine revelation. To the contrary, Acts presents Paul as one commissioned by the community. Further, Acts reports a separation between Paul and Barnabas resulting over their disagreement about a suitable traveling companion (15:36-41).

Conclusion

As one side of an ancient conversation, the high-context letters from Paul can be complex and thus a challenge to understand nearly two thousand years later. The letter to the Galatians never explicitly mentions where Titus was born. It is entirely possible that Titus was from Antioch, though all we know is that he left with Paul from Antioch. We are never told who his parents were or his occupation before he began to work with Paul. Titus is sufficiently identified as a Greek. Assuming there were others in Antioch who, like Titus, were also Greeks/uncircumcised, we are never told specifically why it was Titus who accompanied Paul and Barnabas. Given his later journeys, it is possible that Titus was a good candidate because he had the means to travel to Jerusalem without putting his family or other group associations at risk. Given the mention Paul makes of him to the Galatians, it is clear Titus had been an appropriate companion.

In his recollection of that trip to Jerusalem, Paul remembers Titus not with the labels used to identify an associate, but as one behaving like an associate. Titus and Paul never wavered in their understanding of how respective groups of Israelites could live out the new innovation of what God had done in Christ. Paul never reports himself as having protected Titus or having pleaded with him to understand what was at stake during the visit. To the contrary, Paul simply reports that Titus never submitted to the interest of others to have him circumcised. As an associate of Paul, Titus was not compelled to engage in this behavior by those seeking to remove his freedom. Titus lived honorably aware of a life in Christ.

Paul likely wishes those in Galatia would model themselves after Titus (and Paul) and in distinction to some of those in Jerusalem who never extended Titus the hand of fellowship. As Paul's characterization of others unfolds, this lack of consideration for Titus could be tied to their characteristically vacillating behaviors. What is certain is that the pillars in Jerusalem had recognized what Paul was doing as legitimate. And it seems quite likely that Paul would have hoped those in Galatia who received this letter would likewise recognize Paul's honorable place as their agent of the gospel.

In general, the trips to Jerusalem made it clear to Paul and others that both the particularly Judean customs and the more universally received Greek lifestyles could be appropriate in Christ. In addition, it was determined that Paul would serve as agent to the latter Greek uncircumcised group, while others would serve in and around Jerusalem. While Paul's status or honor is in play at a number of levels in this encomium, one of Paul's primary goals for presenting these two Jerusalem trips to the Galatians was to make clear that Paul's agency was to the Greeks, the uncircumcised. The pillars, by contrast, were in and around Jerusalem as agents for the circumcised (Gal 2:9). Since Paul presents this distinction as something recognized by both Paul and the pillars, it is further likely that the Galatians were being asked to recognize those others who came to Galatia after Paul as persons like the false brothers. They held no recognition or status from Paul or the pillars. They were, in fact, "out of bounds." Yet, they had sneaked into Galatia with their unnecessary demands. By contrast, Paul consistently ties the truth of his gospel to its source and through the honor of its messenger. Exactly who is with Paul and what these persons do, how they behave, is very much central early in the letter. Part of Paul's comparatively superior character or honor comes from his relationship with persons like Titus, persons Paul associates with and praises.

CHAPTER 4

Titus According to the Data from 2 Corinthians

L ike the previous chapter, this begins with an overview of some important features of the letters known today as 1 and 2 Corinthians. The remainder of the chapter is focused on explaining the various roles taken by Titus as he interacted with the group at Corinth. In this correspondence Titus is presented as one who was appropriately received (hospitality) by Corinth, as one to whom Paul had "boasted," and as one considered to be living in Christ with Paul and the Corinthians.

After developing a need to change, the role of a change agent is focused on sustaining an exchange of information, on diagnosing and responding to any problems, and, in general, on keeping the group together, stabilizing the group or, stated in the negative, avoiding discontinuity within the group. Because of the amount of data, the letters to Corinth are especially insightful for understanding the activity of second-generation persons like Paul and Titus who served as agents of change. Several persons are mentioned in these letters as working through early years of Corinthian storming. Timothy and Silvanus are specifically noted as two who had first (ca. 40 or 50) proclaimed Christ there with Paul (2 Cor 1:19). Apollos (1 Cor 1:12; 3:4-22; 4:6; 16:12), Cephas (1 Cor 1:12; 3:22; 9:5), and Barnabas (1 Cor 9:6) are also mentioned as familiar persons. With consideration of Titus (2 Cor) and the possibility that the cosender Sosthenes (1 Cor 1:1) played some type of role there, one has a general idea of the number of persons that could have been involved in helping a group advance through their early development.

Prior to the arrival of Titus, these others may have been involved in a number of challenges. First Corinthians, written about AD 54, responds to issues communicated to principal second-generation agents in written (7:1–16:4) and oral reports by "Chloe's people" (1:11). In general, 1 Corinthians reminds those receiving the letter to refocus on the source or cause of their existence and to foster the integrity of the group over any cliques or factions. Paul asks, "What have you that you did not receive? If then you received it, why do you boast as if it were not a gift?" (1 Cor 4:7). Unlike most questions today asked in search of information, Paul already knew the answer. Paul's questions, like many portrayed in the Bible, functioned more as challenges to those who should have known better, but apparently needed to be reminded.[1]

The Corinthian effort to seek advice or send someone to report problems or concerns indicates at least some in Corinth valued (honored) Paul and his associates. The letter also indicates, however, that Paul and his associates may have been challenged by others in their absence. Paul notes that there was arrogance in some and this arrogance was, of course, a claim to status (honor). Paul's response is both to announce Timothy's arrival and to remind them that while there may be a myriad of persons who watch over them, there was ultimately only one who provided the Corinthians with the initial insight about what God was now doing (1 Cor 4:14-17). And this "father" was Paul.[2] Paul more often characterizes himself as a brother within the network. By employing this other fictive kin term he reminds the Corinthian group of their past. Paul is not suggesting he is the ultimate patron. God is. Paul, however, was one of those who made their interest in the innovation possible. In line with the proverbial childrearing wisdom of the day, Paul stays with this somewhat metaphorical language to further note that if God allowed for the trip, he could return to Corinth with a stick or a "rod" (1 Cor 4:21). What modern Americans would call corporal punishment was not only permissible but assumed to be an appropriate way of provoking collectivistic behavior.[3] Still, Paul knows that would be the old way. Paul could also come to them with a more gentle spirit of concern for the (fictive) family he had helped form. The choice was theirs. In the meanwhile, Paul and Sosthenes write that instead of always holding to the conventional norms of their previous life, a new hierarchy for determining status should be considered. But, such behaviors must be recognized as gifts (apostles, prophets, teachers, etc.) given by God (1 Cor 12–14).

Titus in Corinth

Titus is mentioned in a few different sections of 2 Corinthians. Although this letter appears in the Bible as a single letter, a number of features suggest 2 Corinthians is probably a composite of at least a few and perhaps several letters.[4] Some of these features that suggest the composite form will come into play as Titus is described below.

Titus is not mentioned in 1 Corinthians. His first contact with the group in Corinth seems to have been about the mid-50s. Midway through the second chapter of 2 Corinthians, Titus is first mentioned as a "brother." Like so many others mentioned by the second-generation documents, Titus is described through such fictive kin terminology as both socially related to others like Paul and under their common father, the very God appreciated anew through the raising of Jesus. The initial concern with Titus stems from his failure to have met with Paul in Troas, a city about 250 miles northeast of Corinth on the other side of the Aegean Sea. Sure of his role as God's agent, yet always sensitive to God's control of reality, Paul informs the Corinthians that since a door had been opened (passive, implying God had opened the door), he could have stayed in Troas to proclaim the gospel there (2 Cor 2:12). But, as he could not find Titus, this was not to be.[5] Paul then reports to the Corinthians that he had to leave Troas and travel to Macedonia in hopes of finding Titus (2 Cor 2:13b).[6] Today such information might appear as little more than trivial travelogue. Nevertheless, Paul is relating important and nuanced information about his care and concern for Titus and the Corinthians. Paul was not a broker who simply set up connections and ran on to the next opportunity. As an agent of change, his concern to help the Corinthians remained genuine and a part of their mutual existence in Christ.

Titus is not at all mentioned between chapters 2 and 7.[7] With the resumption of Paul's report of his journey to Macedonia (2 Cor 7:5, not mentioned since 2:13), the report of his reunion with Titus follows (2 Cor 7:6f). But the letter does more than resolve the concern with Titus. Much of 7:7-16 praises Corinthian hospitality. Essentially, the letter reports to the host (the Corinthians collectively) what the guest (Titus) had told Paul. Since the process of hospitality (transforming the stranger to friend or enemy) ultimately reflected the relationship between the community that served as host and the community from which the guest originated, the Corinthian reception of Titus also communicates a positive or honorable reception of Paul and his associates.

As is often the case in high-context communications, details (for example, about what caused the delays to the reunion) are unimportant. What matters is the net outcome. Paul tells the Corinthians that Titus had described the Corinthians through a mere but sufficient list of three characteristics. They were "longing," "mourning," and held "zeal" for Paul (2 Cor 7:7). While these terms are not synonymous, all have to do with expressions of commitment to Paul and thus loyalty to the group. Longing is a fairly direct conceptual translation from the Greek. Collectively, the Corinthians yearned or held a strong desire for Paul. Second mentioned was their zeal or zealousness. This was described above (chap. 2) as one of Paul's characteristics in his letter to the Philippians. He also uses this term when relating his honor to the Galatians (1:14). There the term signified Paul's "total commitment" to one of his initial primary groups, the Pharisees. In this context too, the term qualifies the Corinthian commitment to group, specifically the groups established by change agents like Paul, Titus, and the others. The third characteristic, mourning, relates a different sense than understood in contemporary settings. Today, one "in mourning" might be recognized as displaying an atypical emotional state. Other individualists may or may not recognize or associate that state with the one in mourning. Nor would they necessarily feel obliged to commiserate with him or her. In Paul's day, however, mourning was an event associated with more predictable (collectivistic) behaviors.[8] Wearing sackcloth, appearing unwashed and unkempt, and verbally crying out to God against the evil before them were all behaviors designed for public consumption. These behaviors demonstrated that one in the group had been humiliated and was in need of help (Matt 2:18; Mark 16:10; Luke 8:52). As attributes communicated from the Corinthians to Titus to Paul and now related back to the Corinthians, the words and the larger process all communicate a very general but important statement. Whatever the problem was, things are now recognized to be as they should be by everyone involved.

With the letter's report of the reunion, there is also a justification for a previous letter that had at first grieved the Corinthians but, ultimately, served its purpose. Initially the letter was taken offensively, as to their collective shame. But, they accepted shame and reacted to whatever the issue was. The lack of detail relating to the letter has provided much scholarly investigation. But whatever was said was ultimately not a matter for or about individuals, but about the group.[9] That previous letter is characterized as an opportunity to allow *them* to show *their* "zeal" for *us* (2 Cor 7:12). While the "them" and "their zeal" likely refers to the Corinthians, the "us" is certainly Paul, Timothy, and Titus. But it could also include others "in Christ." Indeed, as the letter will indicate, a goal for the second-generation groups associated with Paul is to gather and send a collection that would provide for those in Jerusalem. As presented to the Corinthians, contributing to this gift would have expressed their awareness of the extent to which life in Christ was possible.

But before unpacking the purpose and meaning of this gift, another social dimension about Titus' trip to Corinth is presented. Paul admits that before Titus left, he had boasted to Titus about the Corinthians (2 Cor 7:14). Whatever connotations boasting might bring today, Paul's collectivistic world tied boasting to the ever-present concern with honor, making a claim to public worth and having that claim confirmed by public recognition. Paul had made a claim about the Corinthians to Titus. Again, we have no specifics, but the context suggests that Paul had prepared Titus to expect favorable (i.e., "in Christ") conditions in the Corinthian community. With the return of Titus and his positive report, it is clear to Titus (in this case, the single member of the audience of public recognition) that Paul's claim about the Corinthians was accurate or true (2 Cor 7:14). Thus, Paul's boasting is no longer subject to shame.[10] If the Corinthian group had not been all that Paul had said (boasted) it would be, Titus could have shamed Paul by reporting his inflated or inaccurate assessment. The language used here in 2 Corinthians underscores the fact that in a collectivist context, Paul's concern was not so much with any inner state of feeling ashamed but with his associate's public affirmation of his characterization of the Corinthians.

At the beginning of this chapter it was noted that a concern in 1 Corinthians was that some boasted. Since boasting is not always a good thing (e.g., Rom 3:27–4:5; Phil 3:3-4; 2 Cor 10:13), it is important to distinguish where and how boasting is appropriate. The concern is seldom with the act of boasting (understood as a claim to worth), but with the need for one to recognize in whom one boasts. Some beings (or states brought about by beings) are worthy of boast. Others are not. In Paul's mind, of course, there is ultimately only one deserving of boasting: the God of Israel or, by extension, what God has touched, moved, or spirited. Paul can and does boast about what God has done. And whatever God does, whoever God calls or provides with some gift through the spirit is worthy of boast as well as thanks. By contrast, if one (at the stage of storming) "in Christ" were to boast as if self-important (1 Cor 4:7), he or she would be demonstrating an inability to appreciate or recognize what it means to be in Christ.

Near the end of this section praising Corinthian hospitality, Paul characterizes Titus as one whose "heart goes out all the more to you, as he remembers the obedience of you all and the fear and trembling with which you received him" (7:15). In English a phrase like "my heart goes out to you" might carry connotations of sympathy. For example, in the context of a recent tragedy one might say, "My heart goes out to you," meaning something to the effect that "I'm sorry to hear this happened to you." In the context of the second generation, however, it continues to communicate this general notion that all (Titus, Timothy, Paul, and the Corinthians) are (in the collectivistic sense) the same. In Greek, the term translated as "heart" really denotes one's innermost self, literally, one's guts. The term had to do with "signifying the seat of one's emotions."[11] Thus, in the context of the day, the term had to do with the self underneath the ceremonial or public self. One can note that not only the terms used to express the self differ from modern expressions, but even the concepts of self are unique.

Our modern ability to think about various organs of the body performing their respective functions within a larger system differs greatly from many of the connections the ancients made. Some literature from the past portrays the person as a composite of body and soul, etc. Documents from the Bible often depict an awareness of three zones that describe the human.[12] Each zone is typically associated with connected pairs of body parts that are thought to work in unison toward a specific task. The first zone is that of "emotion fused thought." This zone is typically described with the pair "eyes and heart." The place for thought, the heart, gets its data from the eyes. The other two zones are those of expression, typically associated with the word pair of "mouth and ears" (and all that is related to these: tongue, throat, teeth, hearing, etc.), and the zone of purposeful action or activity, typically associated with arms and feet (or related features like hands, legs, etc.). While the letter does not contain the typical term for heart, mention of Titus' heart (or, literally, bowels) going out to the Corinthians describes what Titus saw. The letter communicates to the Corinthians that Titus understands that the Corinthian group includes Titus and Paul. They are, at core, together in Christ. In a world so aware of and concerned with the public's consumption of outward normative behavior, these expressions are all ways of telling the Corinthians that Titus the guest considers himself thoroughly connected with the host Corinthians. Hospitality had transformed the stranger into friend and the friend (Titus) recognized as much. Equally as important for the developing communication between the change agent and those adapting the change, Titus reported this to Paul. Now, in turn, the letter reports back to the Corinthians what they said and how they acted as a way of acknowledging the group's honor.

This connection between the Corinthians and others in Christ is also characterized by the fact that Titus "remembers" both their "obedience" and the fact that the Corinthians "received him" with "fear and trembling" (2 Cor 7:15). At first glance, such terminology might suggest that Paul had commissioned or sent Titus as a delegate to Corinth. Assuming as much, some might further suggest that Paul had endowed Titus with power to impose significant sanctions. The language of fear and trembling is also related to hospitality. A previous letter included a reminder that Paul had first come to the Corinthians with his own "fear and trembling" (1 Cor 2:3; cf. Phil 2:12). Such characteristics appear to describe an appropriate disposition for one about to transition from stranger to friend or foe. Further, the notion that Titus was commissioned as one with sanctions is simply not consistent with the general approach of second-generation letters. This will be brought up again below when considering the portrayal of Titus in 2 Corinthians 8.

Concluding this section, Paul makes a kind of public confession: "I rejoice, because I have perfect confidence in you" (2 Cor 7:16). In today's language, such terms as joy and confidence might suggest Paul was interested in conveying his inner emotions to the group. As noted above in the discussion of Paul's letter to the Galatians, emotions are not taboo. In honor-based cultures, however, such information serves as a way of qualifying the Corinthians more so than Paul's inner self. The information informs the Corinthians that Titus and now Paul and Timothy are aware of and rejoice over the fact that all concerned are on the same page. Paul, Titus, and the Corinthians all have the same favorable view of the relationship. The Corinthians are "in" with Paul and others in this network.

Ending a portion of a letter, if not a letter itself, on such a note of confidence would have been Paul's way of honoring the Corinthians. They were brothers and sisters honorably responding to their call by God. Through letters and hospitality, the change agent had successfully maintained a sufficient level of communication so that the group could continue to grow beyond past obstacles. At the same time, expressing such confidence need not be understood as the Corinthians' graduation to a state of "Christ fulfilled" within them. Paul's honor for the Corinthians is like any honor exchange, the latest round in a constant and fluid process.

The Gift

In the current arrangement of the letter, the network's honoring of the Corinthian community leads to a request to put their appreciation of the innovation into action. In particular, the Corinthians are requested to complete a collection of "relief of the saints" (2 Cor 8:4). Most contemporary interpreters tie this collection to Paul's second visit to Jerusalem where, after being offered the handshake of fellowship, Paul and Barnabas were asked to "remember the poor."[13] Aware that this meeting with Cephas and others resulted in many publicly recognizing that Paul was to work with the Diaspora or Greek Israelites while Cephas and others worked with those in and around Jerusalem, Paul pursues this gift as a way of demonstrating this realization.

Of course, Paul had noted that this request to remember the poor was already something he was of a mind to do (Gal 2:10), a kind of admission that Paul and Cephas were working through the same spirit and under the same God. At any rate, this collection for the saints was clearly a concern of the second generation.

It is not clear when or how this collection had been proposed to the Corinthians. Second Corinthians 8:6-11 mentions that the arrival of Titus would help the Corinthians complete what had begun the previous year. Since the end of the earlier 1 Corinthians mentioned the collection as an issue to be clarified, it must have been a concern before that letter was sent. The advice in 1 Corinthians was for the Corinthians to adapt the method of collection advised for those in Galatia. People were to set aside some money weekly (1 Cor 16:2). While not explicitly stated, this process suggests that the groups in Corinth and Galatia were not to rely only on the potential gifts from wealthier patrons. The gift was best perceived as something from all willing and able to set something aside. There is also a concern that the Corinthians consider who would be best to help transport the gift to Jerusalem. Such persons were to be more formally recommended with letters. Finally, Paul notes his willingness to join them if necessary in this procession to Jerusalem. Whether Paul's presence is appropriate is a matter that is left to be resolved later (1 Cor 16:3-4).

After essentially challenging the Corinthians through mention of how much the Macedonians had already provided, 2 Corinthians goes on to describe the collection as a return act of similar kind.[14] The Corinthians are to consider that there had already been gifts from the Judeans in the form of their prayers for others. In response, Paul suggests that the collection was a kind of return gift (2 Cor 8:14-15). Today one could speak of such an exchange as demonstrating a kind of balanced reciprocity between the Greek and Judean groups. In pursuing such a relationship, Paul and his associates would have made it clear that the "group" in Christ is no longer merely defined in terms of physical proximity (e.g., those around Corinth or groups within the province of Galatia). Their transformation to manifest this act was part of a common recognition of a shared (collectivistic) life in Christ.

Paul describes this gift in a similar way in his letter to the Romans (Rom 15:25-33). In general, this letter notes that Paul had already done what he could in the north central Mediterranean area (Rom 15:19), and that he wished soon to stay for a time in Rome before work in Spain.[15] Thus, he writes to demonstrate himself as a person worthy of hospitality. To modern eyes, it might appear that such an ultimate request would not require an extensive letter. But considering the context of the time (no catechism or universally received doctrine), it may be that this letter was even a bit shorthanded. Paul was probably aware that others had been to Rome with information about him. And in the midst of group developments (storming), Paul would have been concerned at least to replicate (or perhaps in certain instances to further clarify) such information firsthand. At any rate, these long-term plans are described as clearly dependent on more immediate plans to visit Jerusalem with a gift. Here again, the gift is described as a matter of reciprocity, something that provides an equal balance between Judean and non-Judean Israelites concerned with the new things God is doing (Rom 15:27). Those in Jerusalem who shared what they had been given as more spiritual gifts could now receive a more material gift. Besides his views of the function of the gift, Paul also informs (or perhaps admits to) the Romans that he and the gift might not be received. Thus, Paul requests his readers pray that he is "delivered from the unbelievers in Judea" and that his service for Jerusalem is "acceptable" (Rom 15:30-31). As always, Paul's concern for honor is at the forefront. And, as is typical, this honor is in play with consideration of more than one perspective. First and foremost, Paul's honor is being forecast to the Romans as something that deserves to be received in Rome and in Jerusalem. At the same time, there is a kind of disclaimer. Because of some in Judea, the gift might not be received.

What produced Paul's concern for the reception of the gift is not entirely clear. Part of Paul's concern may have stemmed from his awareness of the ambiguity of gift giving in the ancient world. Gifts in antiquity could function as a significant medium for creating, sustaining, furthering, and sometimes challenging social roles.[16] In other words, gifts were tied to patronage and, of course, honor. Like honor and many patron-client exchanges, there were no absolute rules for how gifts were exchanged or what they necessarily implied. For example, when elite equals exchanged among themselves, competition could result. In an attempt to protect their social standing (honor), elites would make an effort to out-gift one another. If one could not return a gift more impressive than the one received, it could be perceived as an admission of the superior status of the one who provided the initial or latest gift. This was plausible because giving a gift was a way of communicating to others that the one giving gifts held access to such goods and their distribution, status.

Paul's concern about the "unbelievers" (Rom 15:31) could have been related to a concern about boundaries. As noted in the discussion of the letter to the Galatians, Paul last left Jerusalem recognized—by most—as an equal-but-separate change agent. As such, Paul would have been aware of and concerned about respective boundaries. As the network worked to provide a gift and transport it to Jerusalem—even with the pillars in agreement about the gift, Paul and others would have had reason to suspect that some (e.g., the spies mentioned in Galatians) would perceive the gift as an encroachment or entry into an area that was not appropriate for the network associated with Paul. Thus, in mentioning the gift, Paul takes into consideration how the gift and his role with this gift would be received by any number of audiences. By reminding some in the network that Cephas had requested the gift and by stressing that the gift was a form of balanced reciprocity, Paul can claim to be worthy of reception in Jerusalem. He was not intending to challenge anyone. To the contrary, the gift would strengthen the ties of those in Christ. In the end, of course, there were no legal papers to be drawn up in preparation for transporting the gift or to clarify what it really meant if some were to interpret it otherwise. All Paul could be sure of was that the reception of the gift was a matter for others to interpret.

This concern with the gift is also seen in the interest with having Titus return to Corinth to help complete what had already begun (2 Cor 8:6). Exactly how Titus would complete this work is not articulated. Again, his presence need not be seen merely as a logistical or inspirational force. Titus may have been most useful as one who could explain how the gift was to function for those used to giving within a much more personal circle or group, that is, face to face. At any rate, since all effects are due ultimately to God, there is little surprise in finding the return of Titus as having been divinely motivated (2 Cor 8:16). Further, the role of hospitality would suggest that following his stay in Corinth, Titus was a friend and could have thus expected to be received again if he was to leave of his own accord. As Paul states it, Titus' return is both requested by Paul and voluntarily undertaken. Thus, his return is, like the desire for the gift shared by Paul and the pillars (Gal 2:10), presented as a mutual decision typical of persons operating with the same group concerns. Paul and Titus were mutually interested in fostering this collection in Corinth to completion.

Some have tied the language used in this section to "administrative" language used in Roman business and legal documents. Such parallels then parlay into the notion that Titus returns as the result of Paul's appointment; Titus had been mandated to return.[17] It is important to consider and evaluate Paul's choice of Greek terms but, at the same time, it is difficult for the terminology to trump the broader characterization of the relationship. Elsewhere in the second-generation letters military jargon is employed (1 Thess 5:8; 1 Cor 14:8; 16:13; 2 Cor 10:1-5; Phil 2:25; Phlm 2). These terms don't necessarily imply, however, that the second-generation groups in Christ are like an imperial army or that the persons in these groups are centurions. Nor is Paul an officer commanding the group to military action. To the contrary, Titus and Paul are mutually working toward the same goals. Titus is not under the direction of Paul any more than other members of the network like Apollos. The closing of 1 Corinthians notes that the return of Apollos to Corinth had been requested by the Corinthians and even urged by Paul. But in the end, it was mentioned that Apollos would only come at another time when provided the opportunity (1 Cor 16:12). This negotiation between Paul and Apollos parallels Paul's efforts to lobby for the return of Epaphroditus. While he had been appreciated by Paul, his return was not to be something merely ordered by Paul. Instead, Paul explains it as mutually advantageous to all concerned (Phil 2:25-30).

With the report that joining Titus will be the "famous brother," one "selected" by other groups (not appointed by Paul), there is yet another note about the honor and integrity of this effort (2 Cor 8:18-20). Indeed, these men are to guard against any claims to dishonor that might be cast upon the gift. Yet, before the final plea—itself with a rationale directly related to honor—Paul recommends Titus. Titus is qualified as "my partner and fellow worker in your service" (2 Cor 8:23). At the beginning of the letter, Paul had qualified Titus as a "brother" (2:13). As such he is characterized as no more or no less than others, including the Corinthians and other groups who recognized a common patron or father, the God of Israel. Characterized as a coworker, Titus can still be considered as a brother, but one with certain characteristics. As a coworker, Titus belongs to a group of more than a dozen specifically named persons in letters authored or coauthored by Paul.[18] Yet, such qualifications (rather than titles) do not indicate an office so much as a degree of zeal or loyalty to the larger group's identity and well-being. These coworkers are persons who have survived the storming phase, meaning they have adapted the values and roles appropriate for those in Christ. They are moved to bring others to appreciate the transformation possible through their understanding of what new things God was doing. As such they are persons like Paul. Indeed, beyond individuals, entire communities are characterized as working with Paul and his coworkers as all pursue a response to the life that God has infused in them (2 Cor 1:24; Phil 2:12-13).

The term "partner" appears more infrequently within the Pauline correspondence. The only other named person designated a partner is Philemon. Reading Philemon 17, it seems the qualification was conditional upon his future actions with the slave

Onesimus. The term is also used in the Gospel of Luke to relate the sons of Zebedee, James and John, as "partners" with Simon (Luke 5:10). In both examples "partner" seems to designate a kind of collectivistic sharing. It is also important to recognize that Paul can characterize entire communities as having partnered with Paul "in the gospel" (Phil 1:5).[19] In the end, the term appears to designate not so much any office as a concern with collectivistic behaviors and values. For Paul, this is a life focused on advancing the reception of God's gospel. Titus and (at least potentially) Philemon do this as well, just as James and John had once joined Simon to advance their fishing enterprise.

Given that Titus had been portrayed earlier in the letter as one who passed through the process of hospitality and had thus proven himself to be an effective communicator between Corinth and Paul (2 Cor 7), it seems odd for Paul to subsequently recommend him as a "partner" and "coworker." It is possible that such information would have been helpful for those being asked to receive him again in Jerusalem. Since he was somewhat marginalized during that previous trip, it is not clear how letters from Paul would have advanced Titus as one bearing gifts for those in Jerusalem. Recalling that the letter of 2 Corinthians is probably a composite of at least a few separate letters, it is perhaps best to see such a recommendation as out of place. After having been transformed from stranger to friend, a letter recommending Titus would certainly not have been necessary for those in Corinth. A letter would have added nothing to what the process of hospitality had already accomplished.

Final mention of Titus in 2 Corinthians occurs at 12:18. In this context Paul is concerned with the Corinthian perception of both his own behavior in Corinth (suggested to have been during two previous stays) and that of others in the network who had visited Corinth. The discussion is tied to Paul's refusal of material support, a more typical part of hospitality. The Corinthians apparently had a difficult time understanding Paul's rationale for not receiving the benefits that had been received by others who came to Corinth. Paul had not wanted the Corinthians feeling as though they were the ones to have offered something to Paul. It was, in fact, Paul who had offered something to them (cf. 12:14). At any rate, as the Corinthians would have associated Paul with the visiting Titus and "the brother," Paul asks if Titus had taken advantage of them. It is impossible to see in English, but in Greek it is clear that Paul expected the answer to the question to be "no" (12:18). The model of hospitality (chap. 2 above) noted that one of the essential events that transformed a stranger to a friend was the ability of the guest to never offend his host. So, where Paul asks if either he or Titus had taken advantage of the Corinthians, the letter uses a Greek term that very much asks if they had "played by received rules" and thus never deceptively outwitted or defrauded anyone for their own advantage.[20] Paul asking on behalf of Titus very much implies the connection between the two. They are effectively perceived as being embedded in one another, a process that had begun with Paul's recommendation of Titus and the latter's subsequent stay in Corinth. Since Paul's concern is with hospitality and since hospitality is a two-way connection between the host and the community from which the guest arrives, Paul here makes it clear that he had chosen an appropriate person for visiting Corinth.

After Paul asks specifically about Titus he asks two subsequent questions: "Did we not act in the same spirit? Did we not take the same steps?" (12:18: NRSV: "Did we not walk in the same spirit?"). Again, such questions are not in pursuit of information. Paul probably already knows the answer and is thus challenging the Corinthians to publically acknowledge the appropriate behavior displayed by both him and his associate. At the same time, with his two questions about spirit and steps, Paul is reminding the Corinthians that they are all part of the same group that behaves the same way. Recall that the terms associated with the zone for behavior had to do with hands, feet, walking, etc. Such a question about taking the same steps intends to remind the Corinthians that not only are all moved by the same spirit, their steps (*halakah*, walking or behaviors) are the same.[21] Within a collectivistic culture, Paul is noting that he and all with him act similarly.

Conclusion

The letter to the Galatians and the Second Letter to the Corinthians are the only two authentic documents from the second generation to describe Paul's associate Titus. These documents present Titus involved with issues of freedom ca. 49–55. Applying models of social interaction, it is clear that both Galatians and 2 Corinthians portray Titus as one capable of moving an ambiguous or storming situation forward. Paul's memory of an unwavering Titus on a second visit to Jerusalem (Galatians) is complemented by the more complex roles for Titus presented in the Corinthian correspondence. In both, Titus is presented as his own man. He is neither dependent on Paul nor under Paul's orders. Paul boasts to Titus about the Corinthians and Paul is happy to receive the judgment of Titus concerning his boasts. Perhaps Paul would have urged Titus to return to Corinth, but he was already willing to go. While brief, these concentrated portrayals present both Paul and Titus sharing or partnered in advancing the gospel of God.

Paul has terms to describe Titus. But these are more likely indications of Paul's assessment of his commitment to those in Christ than they are titles that indicate a specific office or limited function. In general, Titus is recognized as being with Paul, aware of the same new things God was doing and under the same God-given spirit. This spirit guides Paul and his partner Titus honorably through concerns with gift giving, hospitality, and boasting. Titus is trusted to report on the Corinthian relationship with Paul. He is also appreciated as one who, like Paul, cares for that community and works to advance its awareness of the innovation.

CHAPTER 5

Titus from the Perspective of Later Generations

According to the fourth-generation book of Acts, people from the island of Crete had already come to Jerusalem for the first Pentecost in order to tell of the mighty works of God (Acts 2:11). Writing about the same time as the author of Acts, yet holding a less universal perspective, the author of the letter to Titus portrays Paul writing to Titus at Crete.[1] Paul informs or perhaps reminds Titus that he had been "left" at Crete in order to see to matters not yet completed (1:5a). Although quite generic, these matters make up the majority of the letter's contents. More striking are the letter's portrayals of its various characters, Paul, Titus, and the group addressed. These differ greatly from portrayals provided by the second-generation letters. As drawn out here, these contrasts will both serve as a conclusion to the previous two chapters and precede a final overview of conclusions that can be drawn from this study.

The formal opening and closing of the letter to Titus are broadly similar to those found in the second-generation letters. Between these frames there are five brief statements instructing Titus of his purpose (1:5; 2:1; 2:7-8; 2:15–3:2; and 3:8b-11). These statements are followed by characteristics of a few generic groups: elder male bishops (1:6-9), Cretans (1:10-16), elder men (2:2), elder women (2:3-5), young men (2:6), and slaves (2:9-10). There are otherwise only two brief sections that provide a rationale for the necessary characteristics given (2:11-14 and 3:3-8a).

As noted above, the authentic letters were characterized as collaborative and concerned with groups experiencing a storming within their early development. These letters sent by Paul and others are always addressed to entire groups.[2] By contrast, the letter to Titus is addressed only to him. Despite their common past, Paul's introduction in this later letter presents a rather concise three-point view of "the faith." This faith is that of those chosen, those who now recognize truth, and those who now act in a manner appropriate for those who expect eternal life (1:1-3). Following Paul's description of the faith, there is simply little else about this Paul in the letter to Titus. There is little that would suggest Titus and Paul had ever spent any significant time with one another or that they were intimate colleagues within a necessary and appreciated network. Instead, Paul directs and orders Titus from an impersonal distance. Far from collaborative, this Paul commands Titus to do everything from resolving disputes to seeing that those under him behave according to very basic expectations. Paul isn't working through an encomium or appealing to past experiences where group experiences were shared and enjoyed. He is simply making demands and stating facts. The group in Crete is to listen to Paul through Titus.

At the end of the letter to Titus, Titus is told only of unnamed others who send him greetings. If Paul had "left" Titus in Crete in the sense of having once been there with him, it is probable that Paul would have come to personally know some of those from Crete.[3] Paul merely asks, however, that Titus greet those who love "us" in the faith (Titus 3:15). And it is unclear if the "us" should extend beyond Paul and Titus. Paul's plan for travel is another kind of distinctive criteria between these generational perspectives. The authentic letters note Paul's desire to travel to meet with others in Corinth, Rome, etc. But the Paul of the authentic letters knew well that what the powers of this world had in store for him would be more determinative of plans than Paul's desires (Rom 1:13; 15:30-32; 1 Thess 2:18; Phlm 22; 1 Cor 16:5-7). At the end of the letter to Titus there is no such desire. There is only fact. Nicopolis is where Paul will be. He had "decided to spend the winter there" (3:12b), and it is only Titus who might not be able to get to Nicopolis as soon as others arrive (12a).

Less obvious than the respective generations' different portrayals of Paul are the characterizations of "outsiders." The authentic letters do not provide much about the others. Even when there is attention, the outsiders are not the focus so much as a contrast to the respective groups connected to Paul. For the most part, it seems that Paul would wish such others simply go away and leave differences as that (Gal 6:15). Somewhat akin to the second-generation letters, the letter to Titus mentions a "circumcision party" (Titus 1:10). Outsiders, however, can also be characterized or recognized through insubordination, empty talk, and deception (1:10). These are to be a concern for Titus, who must (somehow) find a way for them to be silenced lest they upset families (1:11). Similarly, those who find interest in following "Jewish myths" or the commands of men who reject the truth (1:14) are characterized as detestable, disobedient, and unfit for good deeds (1:16). Missing from the later generation's letter to Titus is the concern with how such outsiders might affect the internal storming so characteristic of the second-generation letters. The letter to Titus recognizes some who question, but these are not much reasoned with or appealed to through examples and other proofs. By contrast, those who object have only a second chance before being cast among the outsiders (Titus 3:10).

Other differences between the respective ingroups are more easily distinguished. Again, the second-generation letters were consistently concerned with communicating helps or insights to groups storming or struggling to understand aspects of their new identity. As no group had exactly the same concerns, each of the authentic letters had its own unique issues. But, whether the issue was people who eat meat sacrificed in a public venue or the need to deal with those who desire to adhere to Judean customs, the authentic Paul typically provided at least one example of how preferred behaviors are best adapted. Further, problems addressed in these second-generation documents were to be considered and resolved by the larger group. In good times and when challenged, it was always the spirit that was ultimately recognized as driving the group's existence. And while these groups held a hierarchy of persons, the criterion to establish this hierarchy was set by the recognition of certain gifts (apostle, teacher, etc.) as God's gifts. As a metaphorical body, each was important but none was the head (Christ).

By distinction the letter to Titus seeks to fulfill more established and generic directives. Paul has appointed Titus to make sure the group simply adapts these directives as given by Paul. There is little concern with how the spirit will direct such matters. Nor are those who respond to the directives identified according to their gifts or grace. Instead, their place is addressed and ranked according to the criteria of age and gender. Specifically mentioned are broad groups of elder men, young men, elder women, and slaves. The list of behaviors for any one group seldom includes more than a handful of characteristics. Each group is described with one or two positive attributes that are typically contrasted with a few negatives. For example, older women are portrayed with two positives that frame two negatives. They are to be "reverent" (positive) not slanderers or slaves to drink (negative qualities) and teaching what is good (positive). This good teaching is then applied more practically as allowing for younger women to love their husbands and children and to be self-controlled, chaste, good household managers, and submissive to their husbands. Collectively, all behaviors are important "that the word of God may not be discredited" (2:5). Directives for young men and slaves similarly end with the refrain that sound speech or refraining from talking back or stealing from a master will establish the wider group as ornaments of God, free from the scrutiny of outside gossip (2:6-10). Both the positive and negative behaviors are so generic that it is difficult to imagine Paul needing to explain their necessity to the second-generation Titus. It is further difficult to see how these generic concerns would have advanced any group storming their way through their reception of an innovation. To the contrary, the concerns addressed in the letter to Titus are part of a generic stock of expectations set for a variety of honorable persons.[4] Effectively then, the letter to Titus delivers a kind of catalog of conformity, generically describing Paul's desire for an array of socially received persons acting in socially received roles. Those addressed in the later letter are no longer surviving the world, but expected to fit into it so that any abuse from outsiders would come from some other concern.

By far the most drastic differences between the letters of the second generation and this later generation's view come through the analysis of the respective portrayals of Titus. Within the authentic letters, Titus is one who can be addressed with qualifications like "my brother" (2 Cor 2:13) or "my partner and fellow worker in your service" (2 Cor 8:23). Paul's characterization of Titus' actions depicts no concern or oversight. Paul twice relies on Titus to be his own man, never restrained or put upon. To the Galatians Paul presented Titus as one who was not compelled to be circumcised. Paul had not refused or forbade the circumcision of Titus. Paul simply presented Titus as one who remained free even while in the midst of "circumcision" country. As such, he serves as a model to others wrestling with the same type of concerns. To the Corinthians, Titus is portrayed as one whose absence caused Paul such grave concern that it kept him from his typical interest in serving as an agent of change in Troas. When they did meet, Paul speaks about his joy as he realized Titus was delivering news of Corinthian respect for Titus and Paul. Throughout 2 Corinthians, Titus' appreciation for Corinthian hospitality is clear.

In the letter to Titus, however, Titus is effectively separated from his former coworker. Titus is left at Crete, appointed by Paul who grants his position and authority. To Paul he is a loyal son, one who has paid attention and learned the fictive family trade. The spirit working through each is more of a platitude than something traced to specific accomplishments for either.

This later generation's portrayal never qualifies Titus as one who was successfully transformed from stranger to guest. He is simply stationed. Broadly, his purpose is to move a difficult or ambiguous situation forward. For those on Crete, however, Titus is to be a kind of middleman living out Paul's directives until relief comes in the person of Artemas or Tychicus (3:12). (The former is nowhere else mentioned in the Bible. Tychicus is mentioned only in post–second generation documents: Acts 20:4; 2 Tim 4:12; Col 4:7 and Eph 6:21.)

While some might suggest the letter has a tone of a friendly reminder, it would be a very impersonal reminder. Titus is consistently presented as one who has received directives from Paul to be given, in turn, to others. The directives given are short and to the point. Titus is the object of a series of imperatives or commands that are easily preserved even in the English translation. Titus is left to "rebuke," "teach," "model," "declare," "remind," "insist," "avoid," and (potentially) "dismiss" on behalf of Paul. Titus is not someone who has maintained a decade-long relationship through strenuous circumstances. Instead, he is someone who—in spite of such a relationship—still needs certain fundamental aspects of Paul's "faith" articulated or re-presented to him. The language is more typical of a superior ordering an inferior. Like the young women and slaves, Titus is to act with laudable behavior and teaching that keeps others from making a case against the group. The net effect is that Titus is not to be shamed. The English translation states "let no one disregard you" (Titus 2:15; the NAB and NRSV state "let no one look down on you"). As Paul was an example to the loyal son, so too is the son now to be temporarily an example for others on Crete. The act of imitation is certainly consistent with the second-generation letters from Paul, but the behaviors to be imitated differ.

From the perspective of this later generation, the objective is not to help groups respond to the difficulties of where they are in their reception of the innovation, but to show Paul telling Titus where they need to be now. Further, the purpose for such behavior is so that those on the outside can see those in Crete not as a group enduring in expectation of continual new things done by God but as a group that seems to need to fit into the larger cultural expectations of the broader world.

Another mention of Titus occurs in 2 Timothy. Though likely written from the perspective of the later generation that wrote Titus, the letter claims to be written from Paul to Timothy and from the former's perspective that death is imminent. Paul sees his life as a sacrifice and states, "the time of my departure has come" (4:6-7). The letter then requests that Timothy come to see Paul "for Demas, in love with this present world, has deserted me and gone to Thessalonica; Crescens has gone to Galatia, Titus to Dalmatia" (4:10). All are on their way to places Paul had visited. Only Demas (elsewhere only mentioned sending greetings to Philemon and with Luke, Col 4:4) has been tagged with desertion.

While imprisoned in Ephesus or Rome, Paul wrote to the Philippians (ca. 56–57) praising Timothy as one unlike any other. This letter also notes that others formerly associated with Paul had left to pursue their own interests (Phil 2:19-24). One might wonder if Paul's failure to mention Titus should cast a kind of shadow over him. At the same time, the author(s) of the letters to Titus and Timothy suggest that if Titus had fallen out of favor, these later generations found him worthy of the network. Indeed, here Titus is reported to be in Dalmatia.[5]

Given such different yet ultimately honorable portrayals in the tradition's second generation and later documents, it may seem rather odd not to find Titus mentioned in the fourth-generation book of Acts. On the other hand, if Acts is first and foremost intending to show all Jesus groups coming to "one spirit" or living "in one accord," there might be sense in not including any record of one who, before the pillars Peter, James, and John, was never compelled to be circumcised or, for that matter, offered the hand of fellowship.

Titus in Nonbiblical Documents

This process of modifying the tradition about Titus did not stop with these later-generation letters written as if by Paul.[6]

Other documents never included in the Bible continued to portray Titus with their own insights. For example, a document known as the Acts of Paul depicts Titus praying with Luke after Paul's martyrdom. As they pray, two men from Caesar's court approach. Just prior to Paul's death, these two had been instructed to meet at Paul's tomb the next morning. Titus and Luke were there as well. Unaware of their purpose and fearful of being arrested by these two from Caesar's court, Titus and Luke flee. Eventually they come to understand the men had been seeking not their arrest but baptism.[7] While it may have been assumed by other documents, it is interesting to find Titus here performing a rite like baptism.

Centuries later, around 350, the author Eusebius (himself a bishop) would refer to Titus as a bishop (III.IV.5). Since Eusebius became one of the initial Roman historians of Christianity, this aspect of Titus' legacy was probably hereafter set even though Titus is never endowed with such a term in any of the biblical data.

About this same time, St. John Chrysostom, bishop of Constantinople, delivered a series of homilies on the letter to Titus. Chrysostom makes no distinctions between this later letter and those from the second generation. And, although he is less interested in Titus than in Paul, Chrysostom does note Titus' virtue. He reasons it was because of this virtue that Titus had become one of the approved companions of Paul. And it was because of such virtue, Chrysostom understands, that Paul would naturally have placed a great deal of confidence in Titus. Thus, Titus was, appropriately, given "jurisdiction over so many Bishops."[8] As one reads through the rest of the homilies, it is clear that the virtues of most concern to Chrysostom are not necessarily those so important to the first-century Titus and Paul. Like the author of the letter to Titus, Chrysostom's interest in Paul and Titus is primarily as these two highlight the concerns of his own time.

Like other pillars of the early Jesus movement, Titus would soon come to be remembered as chaste.[9] And by the fifth century, a Latin work known as the Acts of Titus would tell a much grander story of the mid-first-century person that we know through second-generation letters. Attributed to Zenas the lawyer, a companion mentioned at Titus 3:13, this document presents a very sophisticated Titus. He is a man of high status and great learning. The document also notes that it was because of Titus (specifically his family connections) that Crete suffered nothing during and after Jerusalem's demise (8). This document probably set forth a number of other traditions picked up by later writers describing Titus.[10]

Indeed, such accretions have continued through time. About a century ago, a document marked *nihil obstat* and *imprimatur* (official declarations that guarantee nothing about historical matters but do state a book or pamphlet to be free of doctrinal or moral error) portrayed Titus as a "secretary and interpreter." It even fixed the date for the arrival of Titus on Crete to the year 64. While this source is cautious about the possibility that Titus was born in Antioch or brought to the faith by Paul, it parenthetically notes that Titus was "the brother in law of the governor of Crete."[11]

A contemporary reader might understand how such traditions were accepted as part of Titus' legacy before the interpretive insights of the Second Vatican Council had been constructed. It is, however, more difficult to understand the lack of caution produced in more recent documents. For example, the most recent edition of the *Catholic Encyclopedia* (2003) provides a mix of fact and some rather interesting turns of phrase.[12] It states Titus was "replacing" Timothy in Corinth and that Titus "restored obedience" there and "began" the collection for Jerusalem. This is not quite the picture painted in the Second Letter to the Corinthians where Timothy and Paul pass on to the Corinthian community the news that Titus reported nothing but appropriate hospitality and found nothing but appropriate respect for Paul. There is little in the letter to substantiate any notion that Titus had moved anyone to obedience or began any collection. The same encyclopedia article notes that after both were in Crete, Paul later "sent" Titus to Dalmatia. Interestingly, the Bible implies only that he had gone to Dalmatia. The entry closes with the tradition that Titus lived in Crete, died there at the age of 93 (other texts note he died in the year 94 and specifically on the date of August 24) and that, later, his remains (other traditions note only the head) were transferred from Gortyna to St. Mark's in Venice.[13] A more judicious view is provided by Pope Benedict who, in a recent address on Timothy and Titus, noted that further information on any subsequent movement by Titus beyond Dalmatia was lacking.[14]

Tracing such developments returns one to the concerns with perspective mentioned in the introduction to this book. In the early days following Paul's death, the letter to Titus made the effort to portray Titus and Paul in ways that reflected the author's perspective of issues confronting those of his time who followed Christ. Later efforts under the new Roman Catholic empire similarly transformed Titus with qualifications like bishop or chaste as a way of assimilating Titus to others valued at that time.

Conclusions

This book began with a sampling of some perspectives held about the Bible. Whether one's typical encounter with the Bible had been through the context of worship or as a text occasionally noted in secular circles, one focus of this book was to create an appreciation for the insights possible through utilizing a social-science reading of the Bible. The first chapter began to assess the various biblical data that portray Paul and his associates. Primarily using the data provided by the second generation, Paul (as a change agent) and Titus (as a first adaptor and coworker) were two of a wider system focused on bringing news of God's new activities to others and seeking to sustain these persons as groups developing through the storming stage.

In the second chapter, Paul and Titus were considered as persons sharing values and perceptions quite distinct from many of those held by contemporary readers of this book. Their views on how the person related to others or the physical world then served as a starting point for the more specific presentations of

Paul and Titus as they related to concerns raised by groups in Galatia and Corinth. Most noted was the collectivistic characteristic of placing the group before the individual. Similarly, their concern with hospitality was noted to be quite different from the contemporary view. Few today have ever experienced the degree of formal line crossings experienced by Titus and Paul. Nor would many today hold any notion that by accepting one from someplace else one was in fact opening the door to others from the same group. While other things like personal causality, honor, patronage, etc., were considered in distinction to the contemporary culture, it may be the second generation's notion of a spirit-driven fictive kin group as a unit that replaced the more traditional mediated reality of God communicating through the temple that was most foreign to present readers. Though some claim to carry on the ability to prophesy, speak in tongues, and heal with hands, many today prefer to participate in an institutional form of Christianity that is ultimately mediated by ordained ministers. Considered as a whole, the second chapter showed how the Bible is a strange and foreign document even while a part of many contemporary traditions.

In chapters 3 and 4 these basic insights about life in the first century were then applied to the data from the letter to the Galatians and the Second Letter to the Corinthians. In Galatians, Titus is an example of one who, like Paul, would not compromise his freedom in Christ. In particular, Titus would not be compelled to receive a circumcision even while visiting Jerusalem. The implications of this (non)act were then used by Paul to suggest a similar behavior for the Galatians and, at the same time, to bolster his character vis-à-vis others whose character was not so consistent. In 2 Corinthians Titus is portrayed in different situations. Paul makes it clear that he both prepared Titus for his visit to Corinth (boasted) and welcomed him at length upon his return. Titus had communicated the Corinthian hospitality and respect for Paul and, by doing so, allowed for Paul to report to the Corinthian community his own subsequent joy. While probably no longer in its original order, the letter then portrayed Titus as one of a group recommended to travel to Corinth to assist in a collection for Jerusalem. The great care to prepare for and appropriately deliver this gift allowed readers to appreciate this act as something that differed from modern-day notions of charity or mutual support. Both letters presented Titus as an important member of the inner group of Paul's associates. Titus is portrayed with Paul and others as persons who shared a genuine concern for the same values and behavior displayed by the larger group. As such, Titus was an honorable collectivistic person typically putting the group before himself and seeking the honor of the group as one and the same with his own honor. The evidence suggests one's place in the network depended on the quality of one's relationship with those in Christ and not on any office. While the network holds a core of inner ingroup members—perhaps even granting that Timothy was often the closest—initially there were no explicit and specific rules or requirements for participation in such a network. Relationships of the second generation are fluid, not set or ordered on much beyond the common interest to bring the change merited by the new activity of God.

It was also noted that the Bible seldom provides much of the detail that has come to be expected in contemporary descriptions of a life. For example, it is not at all clear when, where, or how Titus initially came to be a part of this network. His identity is sufficiently communicated when he is described as a "Greek" who had both the understanding and ability to work alongside Paul through some difficult situations between about 49 and 55.

Similar to other details manipulated or surrendered by the fourth-generation author, Titus does not appear in the Acts of the Apostles. Titus is not remembered by the fourth generation as acting with one accord. Yet, from the perspective of those concerned with re-presenting Paul, Titus is honored with Timothy as a recipient of Paul's letter. Though not quite like the earlier generation's Titus, he is here and ever after presented as worthy of mention, always capable of moving a difficult or ambiguous situation forward. He can get things done.

So what? Those who take courses associated with religion often expect such courses will provide some boost or improvement to their own spiritual quests. By contrast, most instructors are interested in fostering an advancement of skills or perhaps a re-contextualization of prior skills through an academic lens. This study about Titus offers no magic handclap of spiritual insights. It may provide a model of persons who acted on what they most valued. It may also have provided a clearer look into the earliest generations of our tradition. But with the understanding that the relationship between now and then is only generally similar, one might ask what can be done with persons like Paul and Titus. At the very least one might come to respect Paul and Titus for who they were among the first of many generations of ancestors in the faith. Like the relationship with our biological grandparents, some of their values have been carried on in ever-changing circumstances while others have not. Living generations later, we need not necessarily adapt their ancient bouffant hairstyle or once-stylish leisure suits. At the very least, however, we could make the effort to understand who they were and the circumstances of their lives. Through such efforts we might better appreciate their contribution as we, so to speak, stand on their shoulders. But, of course, what we see is different from what they saw on their own grandparents' shoulders.

NOTES

Introduction, pages xi–xx

1. The Barna organization reports that 92 percent of American households have at least one Bible. Yet, the Gallup organization reports that only 59 percent of all Americans admit to reading the Bible "occasionally." More specifically, four in ten read it weekly, on average just short of an hour. On the other hand it seems people assume to know about what they are reading since another study reports that only one in seven have participated in some kind of study that went beyond simply reading English translations of the ancient Hebrew, Aramaic, and Greek documents. For a convenient collection of such survey information see the brief article by Michael J. Vlach, "Americans and the Bible: Bible Ownership, Reading, Study and Knowledge in the United States" at www.TheologicalStudies.org.

2. Within the Roman Catholic Lectionary, for example, daily participants in the Mass would hear only about a tenth of the Old Testament. And although one would hear something from each of the New Testament's twenty-three non-gospel texts, one would not hear even most of the information from these documents.

3. There is a bumper sticker with a drawing of a guy from a popular board game that might serve as an example. Dressed in a tuxedo and top hat, he is handing out a business card with "John 3:16" on it. The caption reads, "It's your get out of hell free card!" This biblical verse that states "For God so loved the world that he gave his only Son, that whoever believes in him should not perish but have eternal life" is the "get out of hell" message.

4. For greater insight into the critical role slavery played in the first-century Roman world see the study by S. Scott Bartchy, *First-Century Slavery and 1 Corinthians 7:21* SBLDS 11 (Missoula, MT: SBL, 1973). Those new to the study of Scripture would especially appreciate the informative and very readable conclusion on pages 173–83.

5. John J. Pilch, *Stephen: Paul and the Hellenist Israelites*, Paul's Social Network: Brothers and Sisters in Faith (Collegeville, MN: Liturgical Press, 2008), xxi.

6. John H. Elliot, *What is Social Science Criticism?* Guides to Biblical Scholarship New Testament Series (Minneapolis, MN: Fortress Press, 1993), 7.

7. These might be mapped out with consideration for something like "Bloom's taxonomy" or through the consideration of developmental stages. William G. Perry Jr., *Forms of Intellectual and Ethical Development in the College Years: A Scheme* (New York: Holt, Rinehart and Winston, 1972). Those not familiar with these or similar hierarchies in designing a sequence of study might think of one's experience with math. A person is better equipped to explore algebra after mastering basic math. Likewise, algebra is best prior to or coterminous with trigonometry and before continuing on with calculus or, perhaps, even more abstract or theoretical math. By contrast, one might think of the varying sets of skills and dispositions associated with reading the Bible along various continuums. A "skills continuum" would find people either very aware of the content of the Bible and various methods used to interpret it or unaware of both content and interpretive strategies. At one end of a "disposition continuum," one might think of people who assume the Bible has no value in today's modern world. Such persons might be further interested in avoiding the Bible at all costs. Or, they might view it as worth exploring along the lines of some cultural artifact. On the other end, there are people who hold the Bible as the ultimate source of meaning and values. Some on this end might have great interest in finding out what they can about the biblical document. Others might be sure they know what "the Bible" means and thus would not need to read it or may be happy to continue to read it only uncritically.

Chapter 1, pages 1–19

1. There are minor exceptions. Hebrews 13:23 mentions "our brother Timothy." Second Peter 3:15-16 also mentions "beloved brother Paul." It may be that some of the other documents like those associated with the names John, Jude, or James originated in different regions. At any rate, there is either no interest or relatively little interest in Paul's network in three letters from John, two from Peter, Jude, James, Revelation, and Hebrews.

2. As they are intermixed, read only a line at a time or as part of a lectionary, these documents can be read as if from the same person. The identification of seven books as deriving from Paul, however, has been the norm for most introductory textbooks since the mid-1960s. See, for example, Werner

Georg Kümmel's *Introduction to the New Testament*, trans. A. J. Mattill Jr. (Nashville, TN: Abingdon, 1966), 178.

3. Pseudepigraphic literally means false writing; however, these are not understood to have been forged so much as written as a way to honor the work of the predecessor after which the later work has been named.

4. Five of the seven letters written by Paul are cowritten or cosent with others explicitly named. These persons are involved with the respective communities to differing degrees. First Corinthians is from Paul and the otherwise little-known Sosthenes. By contrast, 2 Corinthians, Philemon, and Philippians are sent by Paul and his principal coworker Timothy. First Thessalonians mentions both Timothy and Silvanus. Others within Paul's network—like Titus, Apollos, Euodia, Syntyche, Clement, Aquila, Phoebe, or Barnabas—were not involved in writing letters, but they appear to have been very much involved in sustaining the information exchange with the various Jesus groups. The circumstances surrounding the two exceptions to such collaboration, the letter to the Romans and the letter to the Galatians, are significant enough to warrant sole authorship. These will be discussed further below. For now it can be simply noted that Romans has much to do with Paul's personal travel plans while Galatians was a more personal defense.

5. For an introduction and overview of the contrasting points between the authentic and later pseudepigraphic letters, see Dennis C. Duling, *The New Testament: History, Literature, and Social Context*, 4th ed. (Belmont, CA: Thomson/Wadsworth, 2003), 260–91 (for 2 Thessalonians, Colossians, Ephesians, and Hebrews) and 480–89 (for 1 and 2 Timothy and Titus). For tensions between Acts and the letters of Paul, see Bart Ehrman, *The New Testament: A Historical Introduction to the Early Christian Writings*, 3rd ed. (New York: Oxford Press, 2004), 288–91.

6. See Bruce J. Malina, *Timothy: Paul's Closest Associate*, Paul's Social Network: Brothers and Sisters in Faith (Collegeville, MN: Liturgical Press, 2008), 23–47. This model was initially proposed in work done by the historian Marcus Hansen. Subsequently, Hansen's work was expanded by sociologist Will Herberg and more recently applied to the New Testament documents by Malina. There is no notion that all groups must have generations with exactly parallel experiences. It merely shows what can and often does happen in response to significantly critical events.

7. See "Coalition/faction" in Bruce J. Malina and Richard L. Rohrbaugh, *Social-Science Commentary on the Synoptic Gospels*, 2nd ed. (Minneapolis, MN: Fortress Press, 2003), 342–43.

8. One might note how Mark's presentation characterizes the Roman official Pilate as he "wondered" about Jesus (Mark 15:5). By contrast, Luke's

fourth-generation Pilate declares Jesus as *not* acting in a way "deserving death" (Luke 23:22). For more on the social role of crucifixion, see K. C. Hanson and Douglas E. Oakman, *Palestine in the Time of Jesus: Social Structures and Social Conflicts*, 2nd ed. (Minneapolis, MN: Fortress Press, 2008), 90f.

9. Malina, *Timothy*, 31.

10. At times, portions of some of the second-generation letters are concerned with these and other persons in Jerusalem who had come to be displaced by their adaption of a slightly different response to the awareness of what new things God was doing (Rom 15:25-33; Gal 2:10; 1 Cor 16:1-2; 2 Cor 8:20-21. More on this response will be provided below in chap. 4).

11. See, for example, Isa 45:1 where the foreign King Cyrus is mentioned as having been anointed by God even though he does not know the Israelite God. Similarly, even though God had decided to remove the kingdom from Saul, David would still speak of him as God's anointed in 2 Sam 1:14.

12. There are a variety of circumstances that led to successive groups of Israelites being removed from the area around Jerusalem. These exiles or dispersions began in the eighth century BC. The most popular expulsion is that by the Babylonians. This followed the capture of Jerusalem and the destruction of the temple there around 586 BC. But as political situations shifted, dispersions occurred before and after these central events. There is very little data with which to characterize the variety of communities formed as a result of these exiles or dispersions. Paul notes Israelite groups existed throughout the Mediterranean region from Jerusalem to Spain. His data, however, is often not considered relevant by scholars when discussing Israelites or, as is more often their characterization, Jews. The assumption here is that all of these groups did not function with the same customs or behaviors or, for that matter, hold the same views of the temple.

13. As Paul notes this directive, he mentions it not for the sake of listing what he knows the Lord had commanded, but only as these memories apply to the concerns of those receiving the letter. Paul never explicitly states how he came to know this bit of information, but his general notion is that his gospel is from God and that it was given to him only after God had raised Jesus from the dead. As part of the fourth-generation "tie together" perspective of Luke, the notion that one can have his or her needs provided for becomes one piece of Jesus' parting directions to the mission of the seventy (Luke 10:7). These seventy are not a concern of the third-generation gospels but would seem to be Luke's way of accounting for the obvious influence of others who traveled beyond the areas visited by the twelve.

14. The Greek term *ethnos* denotes a body of persons united by kinship, culture, and common traditions. See Frederick William Danker, ed., *A Greek-*

English Lexicon of the New Testament and Other Early Christian Literature, 3rd ed., BDAG (Chicago, IL: University of Chicago Press, 2000), 276.

15. To cite some specific examples, one might notice how both Peter and Paul heal one who had been lame from birth (Peter at 3:1-10 and Paul at 14:8-18), both perform a "noncontact" healing (Peter at 5:12-16 and Paul at 19:11-12), and both raise people from the dead (Peter raises Tabitha at 9:36-43 and Paul raises Eutychus at 20:7-12). In addition, both are arrested for acts concerning the temple (Peter for preaching and healing at 4:1-4 and Paul for bringing a Greek in at 21:27-36). Both deliver speeches before authorities (Peter before the Jerusalem Sanhedrin at 4:8-12 and Paul before Governor Felix at 24:10-21). Both exorcise "spirits" (Peter at 5:16 and Paul at 16:16-18) and both are portrayed confronting "magicians" or sorcerers (Peter confronts Simon at 8:9-24 and Paul confronts Elymas at 13:8-12). Other events tie the two apostles together but not necessarily to Jesus. As a result of confusion, both apostles are worshiped as gods (Peter by Cornelius at 10:24-33 and Paul by a larger number of people at Lystra 14:8-18). Both apostles are imprisoned and then are released from prison as the result of wondrous phenomena (Peter from a Jerusalem prison by angels 12:6-19 and Paul from a Philippi prison after an earthquake 16:25-34).

16. See Bruce J. Malina and John J. Pilch, *Social-Science Commentary on the Letters of Paul* (Minneapolis, MN: Fortress Press, 2006), 335. Also, Malina, *Timothy*, 53–62.

17. Malina, *Timothy*, 63. See also 62–66 for other characteristics of those like Titus, Timothy, and other close associates. See also Malina and Pilch, *Social-Science Commentary on the Letters of Paul*, 348–49.

18. See Bruce J. Malina, "Early Christian Groups: Using Small Group Formation Theory to Explain Christian Organizations" in *Modeling Early Christianity: Social-Scientific Studies of the New Testament in Its Context*, ed. Philip Esler (London: Routledge, 1995), 96–113.

19. What exactly this gospel "contained" is unclear. It was certainly grounded in the awareness that God had done something new in raising Jesus from death. But the notion that it resembled something like the documents that would come to be written decades later by those of the third generation is difficult to substantiate.

Chapter 2, pages 20–37

1. Bruce J. Malina, *Timothy: Paul's Closest Associate*, Paul's Social Network: Brothers and Sisters in Faith (Collegeville, MN: Liturgical Press, 2008), 5–8.

2. Bruce J. Malina, *The New Testament World: Insights from Cultural Anthropology*, 3rd rev. ed. (Louisville, KY: Westminster John Knox Press, 2001), 102. For more on the concept, see 100–104.

3. For a very readable expansion on the patron-client relationship see K. C. Hanson and Douglas E. Oakman, *Palestine in the Time of Jesus: Social Structures and Social Conflicts*, 2nd ed. (Minneapolis, MN: Fortress Press, 2008), 65–80 or the references cited therein.

4. See Dennis C. Duling's brief overview "Social and Economic Conditions under the Romans and Herodians," in *The New Testament: History, Literature, and Social Context*, 4th ed. (Belmont, CA: Thomson/Wadsworth, 2003), 15–19 and, in particular, the helpful graph on 17.

5. Clifford Geertz, "'From the Native's Point of View': On the Nature of Anthropological Understanding," in *Meaning and Anthropology*, ed. Keith H. Basso and Henry A. Selby, 221–37 (Albuquerque: University of New Mexico Press, 1976), 225.

6. By contrast, the fourth generation implies that news about Jesus had spread to "every nation under heaven" just days after his death (Acts 2:5). Note also that Paul never explicitly states his itinerary (minor exceptions exist, for example, Rom 15:24f.) as anything nearly as organized as the three journeys often derived from the book of Acts.

7. This phenomenon was previously articulated by Julian A. Pitt-Rivers and more recently adapted to the New Testament documents by Bruce J. Malina, "The Received View and What It Cannot Do: III John and Hospitality," *Semeia* 35 (1986): 171–89. The process of hospitality is outlined on 181–88. One could also read "hospitality" in *Handbook of Biblical Social Values*, ed. John J. Pilch and Bruce J. Malina (Peabody, MA: Hendrickson Publishers, 1998), 115–18.

8. This concern is found throughout the Bible (Gen 19:1-10; Luke 7:36-50; etc.). Despite more recent psychological readings of Genesis 2, even the story of Adam and Eve in the Garden of Eden basically demonstrates the concern with how guests are to behave according to the expectations of the host, a situation all the more noteworthy as God is portrayed as a king.

9. See Howard Eilberg-Schwartz, "The Fruitful Cut: Circumcision and Israel's Symbolic Language of Fertility, Descent, and Gender" in *The Savage in Judaism: An Anthropology of Israelite Religion and Ancient Judaism*, 141–76 (Bloomington: Indiana University Press, 1990). Eilberg-Schwartz notes that as a rite, circumcision is polysemous, meaning that it has the potential for different meanings to be held by different perspectives through time or possibly even at the same time. Of course, these meanings cannot be anything. At one time circumcision marked "the fertility of the initiate as well as his entrance into and ability to perpetuate a lineage of male descendants"

(143f.), and this suggests the act symbolized or perhaps mirrored similar pruning in nature that allowed for greater productivity. This perspective differs from the pervasive assumption that it was merely an arbitrary sign of the covenant between God and Israel. It is important to recognize that the Old Testament contains several covenants (Exod 19–24; 34; Deut 9; Josh 24) and is, furthermore, far from monolithic about the correlation between circumcision and any "sign of the covenant." Certainly the ancient authors of Genesis 17 would not understand circumcision as a sign of the covenant if the adolescent Ishmael was first circumcised and then excluded from the covenant to Abraham (Gen 17:18-22). Other documents from the Old Testament portray circumcision as something necessarily done on the eighth day, the first day marking the passing of the most severe blood "contamination" from the birth. Thus, on the eighth day, the mother could appear publicly while her son was recognized by the father. Also, the book of Exodus notes the connection between circumcision and one's ability to participate in the Passover (Exod 12:44-48). Living great distances from Jerusalem, Diaspora Israelites probably heard news about the temple and some of the controversies with its priesthood. How much physical contact was possible for the festival or the rite that prepared for it, however, could have come under significant revision even in the centuries prior to its destruction.

10. Shaye J. D. Cohen, "Crossing the Boundary and Becoming a Jew," *Harvard Theological Review* 82, no. 1 (1989): 13–33. "A gentile who engaged in 'judaizing' behavior may have been regarded as a Jew by gentiles, but as a gentile by Jews. A gentile who was accepted as a proselyte by one community may not have been so regarded by another" (14). Cohen also cites evidence of Jewish behavior like lighting lamps and fasting being practiced by non-Jewish Romans in the first century before and after Jesus and notes "in the eyes of gentiles, a non-Jew who observes any of the Jewish laws, even those that have no social component, is engaging in Jewish behavior" (20).

11. See Bruce J. Malina and John J. Pilch, *Social-Science Commentary on the Letters of Paul* (Minneapolis, MN: Fortress Press, 2006), 386–87.

12. Frederick William Danker, ed., *A Greek-English Lexicon of the New Testament and Other Early Christian Literature*, 3rd ed., BDAG (Chicago, IL: University of Chicago Press, 2000), 427. Danker defines the underlying Greek as signifying one who is "marked by a sense of dedication" or as one who holds an "intense positive interest in something."

13. For a comprehensive list with insight into how these function see John J. Pilch, *Visions and Healing in the Acts of the Apostles: How the Early Believers Experienced God* (Collegeville, MN: Liturgical Press, 2004).

14. The fourth-generation gospel adds to the third generation's characterization of such encounters by describing a vision on the road to Emmaus (Luke 24:13-35), an additional voice from heaven (Luke 9:35), and Jesus' own view of Satan falling "like lightning from heaven" (Luke 10:18), to name a few.

15. John J. Pilch, *Stephen: Paul and the Hellenist Israelites*, Paul's Social Network: Brothers and Sisters in Faith (Collegeville, MN: Liturgical Press, 2008), 65.

16. Even within the contemporary Catholic Church anyone who claims to have experienced something as extraordinary as a revelation would have the content of that revelation assessed. If it were consistent with what has already been revealed it would qualify as worthy of further scrutiny. If it were beyond revelation as understood, it would be dismissed as something other than a revelation.

17. For a more descriptive breakdown of the altered states of consciousness and how those who experience them are typically portrayed see Pilch, *Stephen*, 52–55 or the references cited there.

18. These bring details that not only make each version distinctive but also portray a fairly significant conversation that includes both Jesus questioning Paul's persecution and then commissioning him to new efforts. These then become the basis for additional adaptations and augmentations (Paul nowhere is reported to have fallen off a horse or any other four-legged animal) by later venues including expanded stories and paintings.

Chapter 3, pages 38–56

1. See, for example, the introduction to Galatians by Dennis C. Duling, *The New Testament: History, Literature, and Social Context*, 4th ed. (Belmont, CA: Thomson/Wadsworth, 2003), 219–30, esp. 221.

2. Whether an ethnic group that immigrated in the late fourth century BC (sometimes called the northern theory) or an ethnically mixed group of persons who came to reside in the recently created (AD 25) Roman province of Galatia (sometimes called the southern theory), the Galatians were a group to the north of Tarsus, Paul's former home. A map of the area would show that both the Galatians and Tarsus were near Antioch, a site mentioned in Paul's letter to the Galatians. East and south of this area was the Roman province of Syria. The southernmost extent of Syria included Judea, the name Greeks and Romans gave to the area around the seat of the former kingdom of Judah. Of course, Judea's most famous city was Jerusalem, another important location mentioned in the letter.

3. The verb can be translated either as a passive or as a "middle." English translations often choose to morph the "middle" sense of the verb (woodenly, you turned yourselves) to a pair of present participles: "I am astonished that *you are* so quickly *deserting* the one who called you in the grace of Christ *and are turning* to a different Gospel" (NRSV; emphasis added).

4. Hans Dieter Betz, *Galatians: A Commentary on Paul's Letter to the Churches in Galatia* (Philadelphia, PA: Fortress Press, 1979), 49–50, notes the underlying Greek terms have to do with insurrection or political turmoil.

5. The aspects of a life typically included in such a form are listed in Bruce J. Malina and Jerome H. Neyrey, *Portraits of Paul: An Archaeology of Ancient Personality* (Louisville, KY: Westminster John Knox Press, 1996), 23–51, and also noted in Malina and Pilch, *Social-Science Commentary on the Letters of Paul* (Minneapolis, MN: Fortress Press, 2006), 177f.

6. Isaiah and Jeremiah both announce to God's people that God was no longer to be perceived as a protector, but was, in fact, the one allowing for the punishment of his people. Jacob/Israel is presented as one who marks the transition of the identity of God's people from a single family to a broadening collection of families or tribes.

7. Frank Matera, *Galatians*, ed. Daniel J. Harrington, Sacra Pagina Series (Collegeville, MN: Liturgical Press, 1992), 61. This scenario is then associated with Paul's reference in 2 Corinthians 11:32 more fully developed in the fourth-generation book of Acts.

8. Some suggest the underlying Greek term for the visit conveys Paul's awareness that it was a more informal visit. Others take the verb as an indication that Paul was in Jerusalem finding out about things. This latter connotation is then sometimes parlayed into an understanding that Paul went to Jerusalem to study under Peter. These dictionary meanings are best matched with Paul's insistence that the Jerusalem elite, of which Cephas is one, added nothing to him, a notion that parallels Paul's repeated assertion that the gospel is not human but divine. Altogether there is little evidence to substantiate Paul as Peter's disciple.

9. By contrast, Acts 9:26-31 presents an initial trip to Jerusalem where Paul is seeking to join the disciples. "All" are afraid of him until Barnabas declares to them how Paul had spoken in the name of Jesus while at Damascus. Once beyond their fear, Paul is said to have gone in and out among them in Jerusalem "preaching boldly in the name of the Lord."

10. Basing his rationale on the typical use of the Greek, Matera notes a degree of separation between Barnabas who went "with" Paul and Titus who Paul "took along": "Paul's language indicates that Titus accompanied Paul and Barnabas as a subordinate" (*Galatians*, 72). It is possible, however, that the aorist active participle (first-person singular) conveys the notion

that Titus was one "along with" Paul. Frederick William Danker notes that the term relates to one taken along as an adjunct (*A Greek-English Lexicon of the New Testament and Other Early Christian Literature*, 3rd ed., BDAG [Chicago, IL: University of Chicago Press, 2000], 958).

11. This metaphor of running comes up later in the letter where Paul notes that the Galatians had been "running well" (5:7a). Immediately after such praise, Paul then asks the Galatians who it is that has prevented them from being persuaded by truth and declares that it certainly was not the one who called them (5:7b-8).

12. Danker, *A Greek-English Lexicon*, 60.

13. Philip Esler, *Galatians*, New Testament Readings (New York: Routledge, 1998), 132f. Esler notes that "James, Cephas and John condescend to Paul and Barnabas by acting as if they are in a superior position to them in a conflict and are graciously offering a cessation of hostilities."

Chapter 4, pages 57–73

1. When asked of the Corinthians, Paul would have expected their response to this challenge to move them either to recall that their gifts are always to be appreciated as having come ultimately from God or to provide some other answer. Of course, any other answer would have been a public confession that they no longer considered themselves to be in Christ, but held some other view of how everything holds together. For other examples of questions that serve as challenges, see Galatians 2:14; Luke 5:21-34; 6:1-11; 10:40; 14:1-6; 20:1-8, 21-26; etc.

2. It has become almost cliché for some to equate Jesus' references to God as "father" as a sign of intimacy. Given the pervasiveness of the patron-client culture, it would be negligent to ignore the fact that this term also signifies God as "gifter" to the community gifted (grace). And there is no certainty that those who gifted did so with the intimate behaviors one would associate with a biological father.

3. For examples, see Proverbs 10:13; 13:24; 14:3; 22:15; 23:13; 29:15.

4. See Dennis C. Duling, *The New Testament: History, Literature, and Social Context*, 4th ed. (Belmont, CA: Thomson/Wadsworth, 2003), 205–6. The point here is not to suggest that 2 Corinthians is not possible to read in its current form. It reads with less tension, however, when seen as a composite. While these tensions will be pointed out, the concern here is primarily with understanding how Titus functions, not the specific sequence of events in his life.

5. Many English translations attribute Paul's motivation to leave Troas to the fact that his "*mind* could not rest" (2 Cor 2:13a; also, NRSV; emphasis added). Paul writes, however, that it was his *spirit* that could not rest, not merely the mind. As translated, there seems to be a concern to protect God's spirit from Paul's (presumably weaker) human mind. In Paul's world, the spirit that caused unrest could be from the same God who had opened a door in Troas.

6. Paul's trip to Macedonia serves to tie the Corinthian community to those in that province. This relationship will be further highlighted after Paul reports his reunion with Titus. It is interesting to note that while later generations will report Paul (Acts 16:8-11; 20:5-6) or associates (2 Tim 4:13) in Troas, the order of events in these later texts reflect nothing of the sequence mentioned by the authentic letters of Paul.

7. In its present form, the material that interrupts the story of Paul and Titus is focused on Paul's honor. Some associated with Corinth might have claimed that Paul worked for his own sake (2 Cor 2:17) or that he was simply unworthy of doing what he did. Consistent with his message to the Galatians, Paul's response is that his competency comes from God (2 Cor 3:5; 4:7; 5:14-20). As 2 Corinthians is currently arranged, Paul's concern with his status (honor) might serve as a kind of justification for the report about the group being "grieved" (7:9).

8. Bruce J. Malina and John J. Pilch, *Social-Science Commentary on the Letters of Paul* (Minneapolis, MN: Fortress Press, 2006), 161.

9. Even when the communication appears to be concerned with an individual—for example, the man who had apparently married one of his deceased father's wives—the issue is what the group is going to do about the situation (1 Cor 5:1).

10. Paul says, "I was not put to shame" (2 Cor 7:14; the NRSV uses the term "disgraced"). Since Paul speaks about not coming to shame in the passive, it is clear that honor was to be affirmed by others.

11. Frederick William Danker, ed., *A Greek-English Lexicon of the New Testament and Other Early Christian Literature*, 3rd ed., BDAG (Chicago, IL: University of Chicago Press, 2000), 938.

12. Following can be furthered with readings from Bruce J. Malina and Richard L. Rohrbaugh, *Social-Science Commentary on the Synoptic Gospels*, 2nd ed. (Minneapolis, MN: Fortress Press, 2003), 419–22; or John J. Pilch and Bruce J. Malina, *Handbook of Biblical Social Values* (Peabody, MA: Hendrickson, 1998), 68–72.

13. Such correlations are thoroughly discussed in Dieter Georgi, *Remembering the Poor: The History of Paul's Collection for Jerusalem* (Nashville, TN: Abingdon Press, 1992).

14. According to Hans Dieter Betz, *2 Corinthians 8 and 9: A Commentary on Two Administrative Letters of the Apostle Paul* (Philadelphia, PA: Fortress Press, 1985), 42–48, the Corinthian audience would have been aware of the differences between Corinthian and Macedonian wealth. Given the apparent political and ethnic rivalry between the Macedonians and the Corinthians, the Macedonian gift was probably set up as an example of people giving to the extent of their means. Such a setup effectively challenged the Corinthians to repeat or outdo the Macedonian precedent. In other words, such a challenge could have been a kind of threat to Corinthian honor (9:4). Paul's insistence, however, is that it is rather an opportunity to show appreciation for what had been given already.

15. See, for example, Paul Jewett, *Romans: A Commentary*, Hermeneia (Minneapolis, MN: Fortress Press, 2007), 932, passim. As Paul's letter suggests, both some of his ideas and some of the people who knew him had already been to Rome. Such a forthcoming letter would have allowed anyone interested in Paul to understand him better and perhaps help in his mission to Spain.

16. See Gary Stansell, "The Gift in Ancient Israel," *Semeia* 87, no. 1 (1999): 65–90.

17. Betz, *2 Corinthians*, 53–72. Betz is very consistent with his characterization of the relationship between Paul and Titus being other than mutual and collaborative.

18. Romans mentions Prisca and Aquila (16:3), Urbanus (16:9), and Timothy (16:21) by name. First Corinthians, coauthored by Paul and Silvanus, mentions Apollos as a coworker. At the letter's end it mentions Stephanas and his household as coworkers and toilers (16:16). Three verses later (16:19) Prisca and Aquila are named as persons who send greetings but are not specifically mentioned here as coworkers. Second Corinthians is coauthored by Paul and Timothy (a coworker). This text explicitly mentions Silvanus, Timothy, and Titus as coworkers. Thessalonians mentions Timothy as a coworker. In the letter to the Philippians, Epaphroditus (2:25) and Clement (9:3) are mentioned as coworkers. Finally, Philemon mentions the addressee (1) as a coworker along with Mark, Aristarchus, Demas, and Luke (24). Consistent with those who facilitate change, at least four of these qualified as coworkers appear to have had the means to travel. Two of these were Prisca and Aquila and the other two were Timothy and Titus.

19. Luke 5:10 refers to Zebedee's sons, James and John, as partners with Simon in their fishing trade. Paul mentions the Corinthians as a group who are partnered in both their suffering and in their expectations in the future.

20. Danker, *A Greek-English Lexicon*, 824.

21. In most dictionaries of the Bible, *halakah* is described as a kind of normative interpretation of the guidelines from the Hebrew Torah or Scrip-

ture. The term comes from a Hebrew root associated with "walking." Again, in a collectivistic culture, those who "walk the same" are those who behave the same.

1. Paul's martyrdom can be dated to ca. AD 62. While less than certain, it is probably about the date beyond which Paul could not have written anything. By contrast, Raymond Brown, *An Introduction to the New Testament* (New York: Doubleday, 1997), 668, notes that 80–90 percent of scholarship dates the text to the late first century AD.

2. Even the letter "to Philemon" (from both Paul and Timothy) is addressed to Philemon as one of several (Apphia, Archippus, and those gathered in Philemon's house; 1:1-2) who are with Philemon. In the letter, Paul seeks a response from Philemon that would affect not only him but also this larger household. That is, what Philemon finally does with "his" slave Onesimus will be judged by that more intimate community within which Philemon daily operates and by the wider community within which the "saints" and others have, to date, sung of Philemon's praises (1:5).

3. Brown, *An Introduction*, 641, notes that nothing from the authentic letters suggests Paul's activity on Crete. Acts 27 merely has him land there temporarily as a prisoner en route to Rome.

4. Nearly all commentaries note these parallels. See, for example, Martin Dibelius and Hans Conzelmann, *The Pastoral Epistles: A Commentary on the Pastoral Epistles* (Philadelphia, PA: Fortress Press, 1972), 5–8, 39f., 50f., etc.

5. Dalmatia is sometimes used as another name of Illyricum, but, more specifically, it denotes the southern region of that province. Paul speaks of Illyricum in Romans. In anticipation of his journey into Spain and in retrospect of a range of places within which he has worked, Paul notes that "from Jerusalem and as far around as Illyricum I have fully preached the gospel of Christ" (15:19).

6. This phenomenon of a person, place, or event taking on a new role is fairly popular in biblical documents. For some excellent and easy-to-read examples see Lowell K. Handy, *The Educated Person's Thumbnail Introduction to the Bible* (St. Louis, MO: Chalice Press, 1997), 49–59.

7. Acts of Paul 11:1-7. For an English translation and commentary, see Dennis MacDonald, *The Legend and the Apostle: The Battle for Paul in Story and Canon* (Philadelphia, PA: Westminster, 1983), 29f. Such texts may be a starting point for some later artistic portrayals of Paul. In order that someone might pick Paul out in a crowd, Titus is once portrayed as describing

Paul as small, bald, crooked legged, healthy bodied, eyebrows that met, full of happiness with the face of an angel (Acts of Thelca 3; for the last part about the face cf. Acts 6:15).

8. Philip Schaff, ed., *Chrysostom: Homilies on Galatians, Ephesians, Philippians, Colossians, Thessalonians, Timothy, Titus, and Philemon*, vol. 13, *Nicene and Post-Nicene Fathers*, First Series (Peabody, MA: Hendrickson, 2004), 519.

9. Letter of Ignatius to the Philadelphians (chap. 4).

10. For example, it is here that one finds the little detail about Titus living on to his mid-nineties. See Richard I. Pervo, "The 'Acts of Titus': A Preliminary Translation with an Introduction, Notes and Appendices," in *The Society of Biblical Literature: 1996 Seminar Papers* (Atlanta, GA: Scholars Press, 1996), 455–82.

11. F. G. Holweck (domestic prelate to His Holiness Pope Pius XI), *A Biographical Dictionary of the Saints* (St. Louis, MO: B. Herder, 1924), 986.

12. Berard L. Marthaler, ed., *The New Catholic Encyclopedia* 2nd ed. (Detroit, MI: Thomson/Gale, 2003), 93.

13. The *Encyclopedia of Early Christianity* (Everett Ferguson, ed. [New York: Garland Publishing, Inc., 1990], 904) notes the transfer took place in anticipation of the invasions by the Saracens or "Arabs" in 823 but that the relics were returned to Herakleion in May of 1966. Other texts dedicated to the lives of the saints might even note Titus' birth date as celebrated on January 4.

14. Benedict XVI, *Jesus, the Apostles, and the Early Church: General Audiences 15 March 2006–14 February 2007* (San Francisco, CA: Ignatius Press, 2007), 132.

BIBLIOGRAPHY

Bartchy, S. Scott. *First-Century Slavery and the Interpretation of 1 Corinthians 7:21*. SBLDS 11. Missoula, MT: SBL, 1973.

Benedict XVI. *Jesus, the Apostles, and the Early Church: General Audiences 15 March 2006–14 February 2007*. San Francisco, CA: Ignatius Press, 2007.

Betz, Hans Dieter. *2 Corinthians 8 and 9: A Commentary on Two Administrative Letters of the Apostle Paul*. Philadelphia, PA: Fortress Press, 1985.

———. *Galatians: A Commentary on Paul's Letter to the Churches in Galatia*. Philadelphia, PA: Fortress Press, 1979.

Brown, Raymond E. *An Introduction to the New Testament*. New York: Doubleday, 1997.

Cohen, Shaye J. D. "Crossing the Boundary and Becoming a Jew." *Harvard Theological Review* 82, no. 1 (1989): 13–33.

Danker, Frederick William, ed. *A Greek-English Lexicon of the New Testament and Other Early Christian Literature*. 3rd ed. BDAG. Chicago, IL: University of Chicago Press, 2000.

Dibelius, Martin, and Hans Conzelmann. *The Pastoral Epistles: A Commentary on the Pastoral Epistles*. Philadelphia, PA: Fortress Press, 1972.

Duling, Dennis C. *The New Testament: History, Literature, and Social Context*. 4th ed. Belmont, CA: Thomson/Wadsworth, 2003.

Ehrman, Bart D. *The New Testament: A Historical Introduction to the Early Christian Writings*. 3rd ed. New York: Oxford University Press, 2004.

Eilberg-Schwartz, Howard. "The Fruitful Cut: Circumcision and Israel's Symbolic Language of Fertility, Descent, and Gender." Chap. 6 (pp. 141–76) in *The Savage in Judaism: An Anthropology of Israelite*

Religion and Ancient Judaism. Bloomington: Indiana University Press, 1990.

Elliot, John H. *What Is Social-Scientific Criticism?* Guides to Biblical Scholarship New Testament Series. Minneapolis, MN: Fortress Press, 1993.

Esler, Philip. *Galatians.* New Testament Readings. New York: Routledge, 1998.

Ferguson, Everett, ed. *Encyclopedia of Early Christianity.* New York: Garland Publishing, Inc., 1990.

Geertz, Clifford. "'From the Native's Point of View': On the Nature of Anthropological Understanding." In *Meaning and Anthropology,* edited by Keith H. Basso and Henry A. Selby, 221–37. Albuquerque: University of New Mexico Press, 1976.

Georgi, Dieter. *Remembering the Poor: The History of Paul's Collection for Jerusalem.* Nashville, TN: Abingdon Press, 1992.

Handy, Lowell K. *The Educated Person's Thumbnail Introduction to the Bible.* St. Louis, MO: Chalice Press, 1997.

Hanson, K. C., and Douglas E. Oakman. *Palestine in the Time of Jesus: Social Structures and Social Conflicts.* 2nd ed. Minneapolis, MN: Fortress Press, 2008.

Holweck, F. G. *A Biographical Dictionary of the Saints.* St. Louis, MO: B. Herder, 1924.

Jewett, Paul. *Romans: A Commentary.* Hermeneia. Minneapolis, MN: Fortress Press, 2007.

Kümmel, Werner Georg, ed. *Introduction to the New Testament.* Translated by A. J. Mattill Jr. Nashville, TN: Abingdon Press, 1966.

MacDonald, Dennis. *The Legend and the Apostle: The Battle for Paul in Story and Canon.* Philadelphia, PA: Westminster, 1983.

Malina, Bruce J. "Early Christian Groups: Using Small Group Formation Theory to Explain Christian Organizations." In *Modeling Early Christianity: Social-Scientific Studies of the New Testament in Its Context,* edited by Philip Esler, 96–113. London: Routledge, 1995.

———. *The New Testament World: Insights from Cultural Anthropology.* 3rd rev. ed. Louisville, KY: Westminster John Knox Press, 2001.

———. "The Received View and What It Cannot Do: III John and Hospitality." *Semeia* 35 (1986): 171–94.

———. *Timothy: Paul's Closest Associate.* Paul's Social Network: Brothers and Sisters in Faith. Collegeville, MN: Liturgical Press, 2008.

Malina, Bruce J., and Jerome H. Neyrey. *Portraits of Paul: An Archaeology of Ancient Personality.* Louisville, KY: Westminster John Knox Press, 1996.

Malina, Bruce J., and John J. Pilch. *Social-Science Commentary on the Letters of Paul.* Minneapolis, MN: Fortress Press, 2006.

Malina, Bruce J., and Richard L. Rohrbaugh. *Social-Science Commentary on the Synoptic Gospels.* 2nd ed. Minneapolis, MN: Fortress Press, 2003.

Marthaler, Berard L., ed. *The New Catholic Encyclopedia.* 2nd ed. Detroit, MI: Thomson/Gale, 2003.

Matera, Frank J. *Galatians.* Edited by Daniel J. Harrington. Sacra Pagina Series. Collegeville, MN: Liturgical Press, 1992.

Perry, William G., Jr. *Forms of Intellectual and Ethical Development in the College Years: A Scheme.* New York: Holt, Rinehart and Winston, 1972.

Pervo, Richard I. "The 'Acts of Titus': A Preliminary Translation with an Introduction, Notes and Appendices." In *The Society of Biblical Literature: 1996 Seminar Papers,* 455–82. Atlanta, GA: Scholars Press, 1996.

Pilch, John J. *Stephen: Paul and the Hellenist Israelites.* Paul's Social Network: Brothers and Sisters in Faith. Collegeville, MN: Liturgical Press, 2008.

———. *Visions and Healing in the Acts of the Apostles: How the Early Believers Experienced God.* Collegeville, MN: Liturgical Press, 2004.

Pilch, John J., and Bruce J. Malina, eds. *Handbook of Biblical Social Values.* Peabody, MA: Hendrickson, 1998.

Stansell, Gary. "The Gift in Ancient Israel." *Semeia* 87, no. 1 (1999): 65–90.

INDEX OF PERSONS AND SUBJECTS

SCRIPTURE INDEX